Essential Grammar in Use Supplementary Exercises

With Answers

Helen Naylor
with Raymond Murphy

CAMBRIDGE
UNIVERSITY PRESS
www.cambridge.org

PUBLISHED BY THE PRESS SYNDICATE OF THE UNIVERSITY OF CAMBRIDGE
The Pitt Building, Trumpington Street, Cambridge, United Kingdom

Cambridge University Press
The Edinburgh Building, Cambridge CB2 2RU, UK

www.cambridge.org
Information on this title: www.cambridge.org/9780521675420

First published 2007

Printed in Italy by LegoPrint S.p.A

A catalogue record for this publication is available from the British Library

ISBN 978-0-521-675420 Essential Grammar in Use Supplementary Exercises with Answers
ISBN 978-0-521-675413 Essential Grammar in Use Supplementary Exercises without Answers
ISBN 978-0-521-675802 Essential Grammar in Use with Answers
ISBN 978-0-521-675819 Essential Grammar in Use without Answers
ISBN 978-0-521-675444 Essential Grammar in Use CD-ROM

Produced by Kamae Design, Oxford.

Contents

To the student

This book is for elementary (and lower intermediate) students who want extra practice in grammar. It covers most of the grammar areas in *Essential Grammar in Use*. You can use it without a teacher.

There are 185 exercises in this new edition. Each exercise relates to a particular part of *Essential Grammar in Use: Third Edition*. You can find the *Essential Grammar in Use* unit numbers in the top right-hand corner of each page. You can use this book if you don't have *Essential Grammar in Use* because all the answers, with lots of alternatives, are given in the Key (pages 112–127). But if you want an explanation of the grammar points, you'll need to check in *Essential Grammar in Use*.

The grammar points covered in this book are not in order of difficulty, so you can go straight to the parts where you need most practice. But where there are several exercises on one grammar point, you will find that the easier ones come first. So, it is a good idea to follow the exercise order in each section.

Many of the exercises are in the form of letters, conversations or short articles. You can use these as models for writing or speaking practice.

To the teacher

Essential Grammar in Use Supplementary Exercises offers extra practice of most of the grammar covered in *Essential Grammar in Use: Third Edition*. Much of the language is contextualised within dialogues, letters, articles, etc., encouraging students to consider meaning as well as form. This book can be used as self-study material or as a basis for further practice in class or as homework. It is designed for students who have already worked through the exercises in *Essential Grammar in Use* (or elsewhere), but who need more, or more challenging, practice. It is particularly useful for revision work.

The exercises are organised in the same order as the units of *Essential Grammar in Use*, and the numbers of the relevant *Essential Grammar in Use* units are shown in the top right-hand corner of each page. Although the grammar areas are not covered in order of difficulty in the book as a whole, there is a progression where several exercises are offered on one area. For example, Exercise 7 requires students to use given verbs in the correct form, Exercise 8 requires them to write complete positive and negative sentences, and Exercise 9 requires them to write complete questions within the context of a conversation. The contextualised practice in the book offers the opportunity for much further writing practice, using the exercises as models or springboards for speaking and writing practice of a freer nature. The symbol   is used where a student is required to write freely from personal experience.

1 Complete the description of Hannah, and her family and friends. Use the words from the box.

Hannah

| 'm (am) / 'm not (am not) | 's (is) / isn't (is not) | 're (are) / aren't (are not) |

'Hello, I (1) ...'m... Hannah. I (2) ...'m not... British. I (3) .... from Canada. My favourite sport (4) .... basketball, but I (5) .... a good player because I (6) .... very tall.

This (7) .... my brother, Josh. He (8) .... interested in sport. He thinks it (9) .... boring.

Mark and Steffi (10) .... our friends. They (11) .... at work today because it's a holiday. It (12) .... Steffi's birthday today – she (13) .... 18 years old.'

Write what Hannah says about her father.

That's my father.

(Steve) ....
(45 years old) ....
(engineer) ....
(interested in cars) ....
(not at work today – sick) ....

2 Rose works for a magazine. She is asking a man some questions. Complete the questions.

ROSE

		ALBERTO
1	What's your .... name?	Alberto Simonetti.
2	.... from?	Italy.
3	.... old .... ?	20.
4	.... eyes?	Brown.
5	.... job?	I'm a student.
6	.... afraid of?	Snakes and spiders.
7	.... favourite actor?	Al Pacino.
8	.... here?	Because I want to visit your country.
	Thank you for answering my questions.	*You're welcome*

3   **Look at the words in the boxes and answer the questions. Write two sentences, one positive and one negative.**

1   Which of these buildings is old?

| The Acropolis in Athens | The Opera House in Sydney |

   The Acropolis in Athens is old.

   The Opera House in Sydney isn't old.

2   Which of these countries are islands?

| Cuba | Scotland | Iceland | Russia |

   Cuba and Iceland are islands.

   Scotland and

3   Which of these vegetables are green?

| carrots | onions | peas |

4   Which of these animals are big?

| elephants | whales | cats |

5   Which of these is expensive?

| gold | milk | ice-cream |

6   Which of these are you interested in?

| politics | music | sport |

4 Look at the photo of a family group. Read the answers first, then write the questions about the people.

YOU: (1) _Who's that man_ ?
MARIA: That's my father. He's a dentist.
YOU: (2) .... ?
MARIA: He's 58.
YOU: (3) .... that ....
           mother?
MARIA: Yes, it is. She's a dentist, too.
YOU: (4) .... ?
MARIA: That's my sister, Laura.
YOU: (5) .... ?
MARIA: She's 30.
YOU: (6) .... your brother?
MARIA: No, it's Laura's husband.
YOU: (7) .... ?
MARIA: Ferdinand.
YOU: (8) .... their children?
MARIA: Yes. That's Ella and Francisco

5 Write sentences using the words from the box. Include some questions (Where is ... ?, Are your parents ... ? etc.). Use each word at least once.

18	I	is/isn't	your parents	expensive
Jim's book	am/am not	an engineer	Anna	where
old	Spanish	at work	are/aren't	how

Anna isn't Spanish.
Where is Jim's book?

....

....

....

....

....

....

....

....

I am doing
(present continuous)

6 How do you spell it? Write the continuous form (**-ing**) of these verbs in the correct list.

| ~~arrive~~ ~~begin~~ come ~~cry~~ dance decide ~~die~~ dig forget have help laugh listen |
| lie live make play put rob start stop swim tie wear win work write |

+ -ing
crying
....
....
....
....
....
....

n → nn, t → tt, etc.
beginning
....
....
....
....
....
....

e → ing
arriving
....
....
....
....
....
....

ie → ying
dying
....
....

7 Complete the postcard with the correct form of the present continuous (**is/are + -ing**).
Sometimes the verb is negative (**isn't/aren't + -ing**).

Well, here we are in Jamaica, and the sun
(1) ...._is shining_.... (shine).
   I (2) .... (lie) on the beach
and (3) .... (watch) people in the
sea. Most of them (4) .... (swim),
but one or two of them (5) ....
(swim) — they (6) .... (stand) in
the water and (7) .... (watch) the
little fish around their feet. A group of people
(8) .... (play) volleyball on the
beach. The sun is very hot, so Julia
(9) .... (lie) with me on the beach —
she (10) .... (sit) under a tree.
She (11) .... (wear) a big sunhat
and (12) .... (eat) a piece of
watermelon. It's a great life! See you in ten
days.
Love, Josie

8 Look at the picture and the description. Correct the mistakes in the description.

Steve is reading a newspaper. The boys, Sam and Eric, are playing with a ball. They are both wearing sunglasses. Pam is cooking chicken. She's laughing because the smoke is getting in her eyes. Jo is standing with her mother and is listening to music on her personal stereo. She is eating an orange. Fred, the dog, is lying on the grass asleep.

1 Steve __isn't reading a newspaper. He's reading a book.__
2 Sam and Eric ....
3 They ....
4 ....
5 ....
6 ....
7 ....
8 ....

9 You are talking to your friend, Barbara, on the phone. Ask questions to find out what she and her family are doing.

YOU	BARBARA
Where are you?	In the sitting room.
1 _What are you doing_ .... (do)?	I'm talking to you!
2 .... (sit)?	On the floor.
3 .... (laugh)?	Because there's a funny man on TV.
4 .... (watch)?	A comedy programme.
5 .... (enjoy) it?	Yes, I am, but I'm listening to you too.
Where's Pete?	In the kitchen.
6 .... (cook) dinner?	No, he's talking to someone.
7 .... (talk) to?	His friend, James.
And where are your parents?	In the kitchen too.
8 .... (talk) to James?	No, they're making dinner.
9 .... (make)?	My mum is cooking fish and my dad is cutting the bread.

I do/work/like
(present simple)

Sam and Marisa have very different lives. Read about Sam. Then complete the sentences about Marisa. Use the present simple, negative and then positive.

Sam gets up early.

(1) Marisa ......*doesn't get up early.*......

She ......*stays*...... in bed until 10 o'clock. (stay)

He drives a car.

(2) She ....

She .... a bike. (ride)

He works in an office.

(3) ....

.... at home. (stay)

He has lunch in a restaurant.

(4) ....

.... lunch at home. (make)

He likes cats.

(5) ....

.... dogs. (prefer)

He plays computer games.

(6) ....

.... TV. (watch)

Complete the description of London. Use the present simple.

London, the capital city of the UK,

(1) ......*has*...... (have) a population of eight million. It is a 24-hour city. Some people say the city never (2) .... (sleep), so it's an exciting place to visit.

There are many interesting things for tourists to do and see in London – the London Eye, for example. The London Eye is a big wheel. It (3) .... (have) 32 capsules and each one (4) .... (hold) 25 people. The wheel (5) .... (not move) very fast – a ride (6) .... (take) 30 minutes. A ticket (7) .... (cost) £11.50 for adults. You (8) .... (not pay) for children under 5 years old. It is better to book your tickets before if you (9) .... (not want) to wait for hours. The London Eye (10) .... (not work) late at night, but it is open every day, usually until 10 pm.

12 There are mistakes in nine of these sentences. Correct the sentences where necessary. Write 'OK' if the sentence is already correct.

1 David <u>take</u> the bus to work. _David takes the bus to work._
2 Go you to the office every day? ....
3 My car don't work when it is cold. ....
4 What time the film starts? ....
5 How many eggs you want for breakfast? ....
6 Does the 9.30 train stop at every station? ....
7 What does do your father? ....
8 I not write many letters. I usually use email. ....
9 What Sue usually have for lunch? ....
10 How much do these apples cost? ....
11 Charlie play tennis, but he doesn't enjoy it. ....

13 Complete the text with the words from the box.

gives them breakfast	6 o'clock	many times	St John's Hospital	bus
wakes the children up	10 o'clock	very tired	20 children	~~a nurse~~

My name is Jennie. I'm (1) ......_a nurse_...... and I work at (2) .... I look
after sick children at night. I start work at (3) .... and finish early at
(4) .... in the morning. I go to work by (5) .... , but
I come home in the morning by taxi because I'm tired. I have (6) .... in
my section. I look at the children (7) .... during the night. Sometimes I sit
and talk to a child. The children sleep most of the time. At 6 o'clock the day nurse arrives
and (8) .... She (9) .... at 7 o'clock. I go home and
go to bed at 8 o'clock. I usually feel (10) ....

You are asking Jennie about her job. Use the information in the text to complete the
questions.

11 ......_What do you do_.. ?   Jennie
12 Where .... ?
13 What time .... ?
14 What time .... ?
15 How .... ?
16 How many .... ?
17 How often .... ?
18 When .... ?
19 What .... at 7 o'clock?
20 How .... when you go home?

4 Paula is in the city centre. An interviewer is asking her some questions about the local cinema. Read Paula's answers first, then write the interviewer's questions.

INTERVIEWER: (1) ...... How often do you go to the cinema ...... ?

PAULA: Usually once a week.

INTERVIEWER: (2) .... alone?

PAULA: No, with a friend.

INTERVIEWER: (3) .... there?

PAULA: I walk because I live nearby.

INTERVIEWER: (4) .... ?

PAULA: £6.00.

INTERVIEWER: (5) .... ?

PAULA: At the back of the cinema.

INTERVIEWER: (6) .... ?

PAULA: All kinds of films, especially comedies.

INTERVIEWER: (7) .... film?

PAULA: My favourite is 'Silent Streets'.

INTERVIEWER: (8) ....

anything – ice-cream, for example?

PAULA: No, I don't, but I usually have a coke.

INTERVIEWER: Thank you for answering my questions.

PAULA: You're welcome.

Now use Paula's answers to complete this paragraph.

Paula usually (9) ......goes...... to the cinema once a week with a friend. She (10) .... to the cinema because she (11) .... nearby. The ticket (12) .... £6.00 and she (13) .... at the back of the cinema. She (14) .... all kinds of films, especially comedies. Her favourite film (15) .... 'Silent Streets'. She (16) .... anything, but she usually (17) .... a coke.

What about you? Do you go to the cinema? Write a short paragraph like the one above.

....

....

....

....

I am doing and I do
(present continuous and present simple)

15   Which is right?

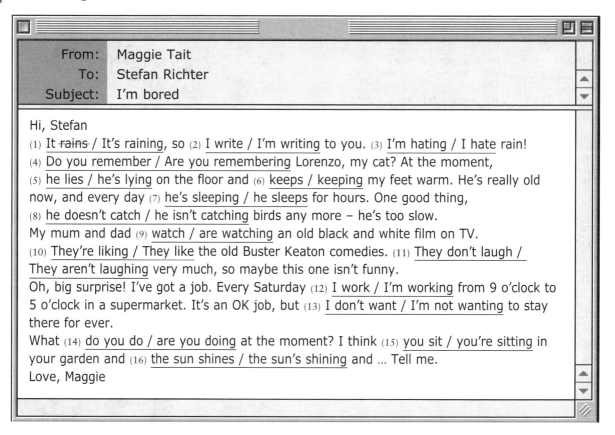

From: Maggie Tait
To: Stefan Richter
Subject: I'm bored

Hi, Stefan

(1) It rains / It's raining, so (2) I write / I'm writing to you. (3) I'm hating / I hate rain!
(4) Do you remember / Are you remembering Lorenzo, my cat? At the moment,
(5) he lies / he's lying on the floor and (6) keeps / keeping my feet warm. He's really old
now, and every day (7) he's sleeping / he sleeps for hours. One good thing,
(8) he doesn't catch / he isn't catching birds any more – he's too slow.
My mum and dad (9) watch / are watching an old black and white film on TV.
(10) They're liking / They like the old Buster Keaton comedies. (11) They don't laugh /
They aren't laughing very much, so maybe this one isn't funny.
Oh, big surprise! I've got a job. Every Saturday (12) I work / I'm working from 9 o'clock to
5 o'clock in a supermarket. It's an OK job, but (13) I don't want / I'm not wanting to stay
there for ever.
What (14) do you do / are you doing at the moment? I think (15) you sit / you're sitting in
your garden and (16) the sun shines / the sun's shining and ... Tell me.
Love, Maggie

16   **Read about what John does before breakfast every day and what he is doing now.**

Every day John gets up at 6.30 and does some exercises in the garden. Then he has a shower. He gets dressed and listens to the news on the radio. Then he goes downstairs and makes breakfast. At the moment John is sitting in the kitchen and drinking a cup of tea. He is reading a magazine and thinking about his holiday.

 Now write two paragraphs about yourself. Use some of the words from the boxes, or some of the words from John's story, or think of your own ideas.

- Write about four things you do before breakfast every day.

clean my teeth	feed the cat	go for a run	read	talk

Every day I

- Write about four things you're doing now.

do	hold	learn	listen to	look at	sit	write

At the moment I

Look at the pictures. Write two questions for each picture. Use the present continuous of one verb and the present simple of the other verb.

1 RUTH: Where ...... *are you going* ...... ? (go)
   JAMES: To the cinema.
   RUTH: ...... *Do you enjoy* ...... the cinema? (enjoy)
   JAMES: Yes, I do.

2 BOY: What .... ? (do)
   WOMAN: I'm a photographer.
   BOY: .... ? (do)
   WOMAN: I'm checking the light.

3 JEFF: When .... usually
                 .... work? (finish)
   BRIAN: At quarter past five.
   JEFF: Why .... now? (leave)
   BRIAN: Because I have a dentist's appointment.

4 LUCY: What .... John .... ? (do)
   PAUL: Reading, I think.
   LUCY: .... a lot? (read)
   PAUL: Yes, all the time.

5 BETH: .... the children .... ? (run)
   ANNE: Because they're late.
   BETH: .... they ....
         school? (start)
   ANNE: At half past eight.

18 Complete the sentences. Use the present simple (**do** etc.) or present continuous (**doing** etc.), positive or negative.

1 (Have a chocolate.)   (No thanks, I ___don't like___ (like) chocolate.)

2 (What ___are you reading___ (read)?)   (A letter from my sister.)

3 (Let's have lunch in the garden.)   (No, we can't. It _____ (rain).)

4 (Where's David?)   (He's in his study. He _____ (read) emails.)

5 (Are Sue and Joe asleep?)   (Yes. Turn the TV off. They _____ (watch) it.)

6 (What time _____ (get up)?)   (Me? About 7 usually.)

7 (_____ (eat) meat?)   (Sandra? No, she's a vegetarian.)

8 (Why _____ (smile)?)   (Because I'm happy.)

9 (Do you like French films?)   (Not really. I _____ (understand) French.)

19 Write questions from these words. Put the verbs in the present simple (**do you have** etc.) or the present continuous (**are you having** etc.). Then write your own positive or negative short answers.

1 you / have / dinner at the moment?
   ___Are you having dinner at the moment?___   ___No, I'm not.___

2 you / read / a newspaper every day?
   ....

3 it / rain much in your country?
   ....

4 you / usually / do your homework on a computer?
   ....

5 you / have / a drink now?
   ....

6 you / drink coffee for breakfast every day?
   ....

7 you / work / at the moment?
   ....

8 students / eat lunch at school in your country?
   ....

have got

Complete the description of Ruth with **has got ('s got) / hasn't got** or **have got ('ve got) / haven't got**.

Ruth is 21. She (1) .....'s got..... fair hair and blue eyes. She (2) .... two brothers, Will and Carl, but she (3) .... any sisters. Her brothers (4) .... brown hair and brown eyes. One of her brothers, Will, is married. He (5) .... two children, so Ruth is an aunt. She lives with her parents in a house. It (6) .... five rooms, but it (7) .... a garden. She (8) .... a small room in the house. In it she (9) .... her computer and a TV. She (10) .... a car, but her parents (11) .... one because they can't drive.

What about you? Write about yourself and other people you know. Write positive and negative sentences for each person.

I .....'ve got long hair.
.......I haven't got a bike.
....
....

My mother/father ....
....

Our neighbours ....
....

My teacher ....
....

My best friend ....
....

Write questions with **got** (**have you got ... ?**, **has it got ... ?** etc.).

1 MARY: Tim is a good photographer.
  PAT: What kind of camera .....has he got..... ?
2 HELEN: My neighbours love cats.
  PAM: How many .... ?
3 PETER: Jack and Sally are buying a new house.
  SUE: How many rooms .... ?
4 DIANA: Tony wants to talk to you.
  ALEX: .... my mobile number?
5 MARTIN: My sister and brother-in-law have been married for six years.
  ROSE: .... any children?
6 TONY: Kate is going to the dentist this afternoon.
  ALICE: .... toothache?
7 CHRIS: Can you write down Jon's new address for me?
  SARAH: Sure. .... a pen?

was/were and I worked/got/went
(past)

22 Complete the sentences. Use **I/she was** etc. or **we/they were** etc.

1 Liz worked very late last night.   ....She was.... tired.
2 Carlos lost his job yesterday.   .... angry.
3 We laughed a lot at last night's film.   .... funny.
4 Joe and his dog fell into the river yesterday. .... wet.
5 Yesterday was a beautiful day.   .... sunny.
6 We saw a horror film on Saturday.   .... really frightened.
7 Paul and Sue didn't have anything to eat yesterday. .... hungry.
8 I had a great holiday last year.   .... happy.

23 Where were you at these times? Use **I was at/in** + a place.

1 ....I was at the swimming pool.......... at 6.30 yesterday morning.
2 .... last Saturday.
3 .... at 7 o'clock yesterday evening.
4 .... last Tuesday afternoon.
5 .... at midnight last night.
6 .... at 1 o'clock yesterday.
7 .... ten minutes ago.

24 Write questions and short answers with **was/were**.

1 MAX: My grandmother died in 1990.
   OSCAR: ....Was she very old.................... ? (old)
   MAX: No, ...she wasn't.............. .
2 ELLA: Jack and Rita had an examination yesterday.
   BETH: .... ? (difficult)
   ELLA: No, ...
3 SALLY: I had a wonderful red sports car when I was younger.
   TONY: .... ? (fast)
   SALLY: Yes, ...
4 DAVE: Mike got some tickets for the World Cup.
   CAROL: .... ? (expensive)
   DAVE: No, ...
5 ALEX: I ran the 100 metres in competitions when I was younger.
   KATYA: .... ? (nervous)
   ALEX: No, ...
6 BEN: Julia wasn't at work yesterday.
   MARK: .... ? (ill)
   BEN: Yes, ...

18

4 Last weekend Judy went to Paris to see her friend, Sarah. Read Judy's diary, then complete the letter that she wrote. Use the past simple, positive or negative.

Saturday 27 June	**Sunday 28 June**
am fly to Paris	**am** buy a birthday present for Mum
have lunch with Sarah	have a picnic by the river
pm go to an art exhibition	**pm** take a boat cruise on the river
meet Chris for dinner	make dinner in Sarah's apartment
go to the Tango Club	catch the late flight home

... so early on Saturday morning I (1) ___flew___ to Paris and
(2) .... with Sarah. Then we (3) .... in the
afternoon. We (4) .... for dinner, but we
(5) .... because we were too tired. On Sunday morning I
(6) .... for Mum, and then for lunch we
(7) .... Unfortunately, in the afternoon it rained, so we
(8) .... on the river. You know I love cooking, so I
(9) .... and then I (10) ....

Think about what you did one day last week. Write a letter to a friend. Use the past simple.

On .... morning I ....
....
....
....

6 A father asked his child some questions at the end of the day. Begin the questions with **Did you ...** and the verbs from box A. Complete the questions with the endings from box B.

A		B	
~~do~~	play	a big lunch	a history lesson
go	spend	any money	any TV
have	visit	football	to school
have	watch	your grandmother	~~your homework~~

Did you do your homework? ....
....
....
....

27 Here is part of a website about the singer Elvis Presley. Complete the text with the verbs from the box. Use the past simple, positive or negative.

be	be	be	~~come~~	die	go	have	have	leave	make
marry	meet	sing	spend	study	teach	wear	win		

Elvis – The King of Rock and Roll

Elvis Presley was born in 1935 in Mississippi, USA. He lived with his parents, Gladys and Vernon. Elvis (1) ....came.... from a large family – lots of aunts, uncles and cousins – but he (2) .... any brothers or sisters. He loved singing, and in 1945 he (3) .... a school singing competition. He also (4) .... himself to play the guitar.

When Elvis (5) .... 13 years old, he and his family moved to Memphis, Tennessee because they wanted a better life. He (6) .... school in 1953 and worked as a truck driver. In the evenings, he (7) .... at night school because he wanted to be an electrician. In the same year, he made his first record, but it (8) .... for sale in the shops – it was a present for his mother. In 1954 he made his first public record and it was a success. People loved his music. They also loved the clothes he (9) .... and the way he moved when he (10) .... During his life, he also (11) .... 33 movies.

Elvis (12) .... into the US army for two years and (13) .... most of his time in Germany. It was in Germany that he (14) .... Priscilla Beaulieu, and they (15) .... in 1967. They (16) .... a daughter, Lisa Marie. The last years of Elvis's life (17) .... happy – he divorced Priscilla and he had an eating problem. He (18) .... in 1977 at the age of 42, but he still has many millions of fans all over the world.

8 Your friend asks you some questions about Elvis Presley. Read the answers first, then write the questions. Use the past simple (**Did ... , When did ...** etc.).

	YOUR FRIEND		YOU
1	Did he have any brothers or sisters ?		No, but he had lots of other people in his family.
2	When did .... ?		In 1945 – when he was ten years old.
3	.... ?		He taught himself to play.
4	.... ?		Because they wanted a better life.
5	.... ?		In 1953.
6	.... ?		Yes, as a truck driver.
7	.... ?		Because he wanted to be an electrician.
8	.... ?		Everything – his music, his clothes and the way he moved.
9	.... ?		33.
10	.... ?		Two years.
11	.... ?		Priscilla Beaulieu.
12	.... ?		Yes, one girl – Lisa Marie.
13	.... ?		In 1977.

9 Complete the postcard. Use the past simple (**arrived, saw** etc.) or **was/were**. Two verbs are in the negative.

Hi Tony
I'm in San Francisco now. We (1) ..... arrived ..... here yesterday. Before that, we
(2) .... ten days in New York. It (3) ....
wonderful. Paula and I (4) .... a lot of interesting places,
including the Empire State Building. We (5) .... to the top – it
(6) .... very high and we (7) .... both really
excited to be there. We (8) .... a boat down the river to see
the Statue of Liberty. We (9) .... through Greenwich Village and
watched many artists at work. The paintings (10) .... expensive,
so I bought one. We also (11) .... to the theatre and saw a
musical – I (12) .... it was fantastic, but Paula
(13) .... it very much. The weather (14) .... OK – a
bit wet sometimes. But now here in San Francisco, it's hot and sunny.
Love, Elena (and Paula)

Now write a postcard to a friend from your last holiday.

I was doing and I did
(past continuous and past simple)

30 Look at the picture. This was Rosamund Street at 10.30 yesterday morning. What was happening? Where was it happening? Write sentences. Use the past continuous.

At 10.30 yesterday morning

1 Rosa _was working in her room._
2 Sam ....
3 Sam's dogs ....
4 Lynn ....
5 Mrs Drake ....
6 Philip ....
7 Mike and Tim ....
8 Felix ....
9 Paul ....

What about you? What were you doing yesterday at these times? Use the past continuous.

10 10.30 in the morning ..... _At 10.30 in the morning I_ ....
11 12.30 ....
12 6.15 in the evening ....
13 8.30 in the evening ....
14 midnight ....

Complete the conversations. Use was/were, the past simple (did etc.) or the past continuous (was doing etc.).

1 POLICE OFFICER: What ____were you doing____ (you / do) when the accident ____happened____ (happen)?

COLIN: I ____was____ at the bus stop. I ____was waiting____ (wait) for a bus.

POLICE OFFICER: _____ (you / see) the accident?

COLIN: No, because I _____ (read) the newspaper.

2 NICOLA: I _____ (telephone) you at 9 o'clock last night, but you were not at home.

MARTIN: 9 o'clock? I _____ (sit) in a café, _____ (drink) hot chocolate.

NICOLA: _____ Jane with you?

MARTIN: No, she _____ (work) in the library.

NICOLA: Where _____ (you / go) after the café?

MARTIN: I _____ (go) home.

3 MUM: Oh no! My beautiful cup! What happened?

ANGIE: I'm really sorry, Mum. I _____ (break) it when I _____ (wash) it.

MUM: How?

ANGIE: My hands _____ wet and I _____ (drop) it on the floor.

4 SOPHIE: _____ (you / think) yesterday's exam _____ difficult?

EDDIE: No, not really, but I _____ (not / write) very much.

SOPHIE: Why not?

EDDIE: Because I _____ (dream) about my holidays.

5 ANDREW: There _____ a crash outside my house yesterday.

MAGGIE: What _____ (happen)?

ANDREW: I don't know. It _____ (rain), but the two drivers _____ (not / go) too fast.

MAGGIE: _____ they hurt?

ANDREW: One man _____ (break) his arm and the other man _____ (cut) his hand.

6 TRACEY: Pardon? I didn't hear you. Could you say that again, please?

DAVE: I _____ (not / talk) to you.

TRACEY: Who _____ (you / talk) to?

DAVE: Sarah.

TRACEY: Oh, sorry.

32 At 10 o'clock yesterday morning, there was a robbery at the Midwest Bank. You are a police officer and you are asking Tim Smith some questions about what he was doing, what other people were doing, and what he saw. Write the questions. Use **was/were**, the past simple (**did you do** etc.) and the past continuous (**were you doing** etc.).

'Now then, Mr Smith, I know you saw the robbery yesterday. I would like to ask you some questions.

1 What / you / do / at 10 o'clock?   <u>What were you doing at 10 o'clock?</u>

2 Where / Joan Turner? ....

3 What / Mrs Jones / do? ....

4 Where / Mrs Walters / go? ....

5 the robbers / carry / guns? ....

6 Where / the big car / wait? ....

7 driver / a man or a woman? ....

8 you / see / a man on the corner? ....

9 some men / repair / the road? ....

10 anyone / wait / at the bus stop? ....

11 you / phone / the police? ....

Thank you, Mr Smith. That was very helpful.'

Now use Tim Smith's answers to complete this paragraph. Look at the picture to help you.

Mr Smith told me that at 10.00 yesterday morning he **(12)** <u>was outside the butcher's</u> .
Joan Turner **(13)** .... Mrs Jones **(14)** ....
with her dog. Mrs Walters **(15)** .... The three robbers
(16) .... guns. A big car **(17)** ....
and the driver **(18)** .... A man **(19)** ....
on the corner and the workmen **(20)** .... the road. Two children
(21) .... at the bus stop. Mr Smith **(22)** ....
the police on his mobile.

I do / I am doing and I did / I was doing
(present and past, simple and continuous)

3 Look at this information about Marco and Jill.

name:	Marco	Jill
age:	15	29
home town:	Rome	Dublin
job:	student	computer programmer
education/study:	12 subjects at school	mathematics at university
likes:	playing football, cinema	travelling, swimming, chocolate
last holiday:	2 weeks in Greece last summer with his family; hotel in the mountains; lots of walking	1 month in Thailand last year with friends; hotel by the sea; lots of water sports

Write questions about Marco. Use verbs in the present or past.

1 _How old is Marco_ ? (old)
2 _Where does he live_ ? (live)
3 _____ ? (do)
4 _____ ? (study)
5 _____ ? (like)
6 _____ ? (go for his last holiday)
7 _____ ? (stay)
8 _____ ? (do on holiday)

Read the paragraph about Marco.

Marco is 15 and he lives in Rome. He's a student and he studies 12 subjects at school. He likes playing football and going to the cinema. Last summer he went to Greece with his family for two weeks. He stayed in a hotel in the mountains and he did lots of walking.

Write a similar paragraph about Jill.

Jill ....

....

....

Now write a paragraph for yourself.

I am ....

....

....

34   Kate and Julia are in a café on Wednesday morning. Read their conversation. There are mistakes in 13 of the <u>underlined</u> verbs. Correct the verbs where necessary. Write 'OK' if the verb is already correct.

JULIA: Hi there, Kate. Where (1) <u>did you go</u> when I (2) <u>saw</u> you yesterday morning?

         were you going
         OK

KATE: I (3) <u>was</u> on my way to the bank.

JULIA: I (4) <u>am usually going</u> to the bank every Monday after the weekend.

KATE: Me too, usually. But I (5) <u>don't have</u> time this week, so I went yesterday.
Julia, why (6) <u>do you look</u> at me?

JULIA: Because you (7) <u>wear</u> something different. What is it?

KATE: It's a new sweater and I (8) <u>was buying</u> it on Saturday.

JULIA: It's a good colour. ... What (9) <u>does Tim do</u> at the moment?

KATE: Oh, poor Tim! He's at the doctor's now. He (10) <u>was falling</u> yesterday when he (11) <u>was running</u> for the bus.

JULIA: (12) <u>Does he hurt</u> himself?

KATE: He (13) <u>was waking</u> up this morning and said his leg was painful, but I think he's OK really.

JULIA: I hope he (14) <u>don't watch</u> that programme on TV last night. It was about new ways of mending broken legs.

KATE: No, we (15) <u>aren't usually watching</u> much TV.

JULIA: That's OK then. Let's have another cup of coffee.

KATE: Good idea. Then you can tell me about Rosie. I (16) <u>go</u> to her house on Friday night and she (17) <u>was sitting</u> in the dark – no lights on anywhere in the house. She (18) <u>was</u> very unhappy all weekend. What's the matter? Do you know?

JULIA: Yes, but hang on, let me get the coffee first.

5 Complete this conversation with film actor, Nicole Casey. Put the verbs in the correct past or present form.

INTERVIEWER: When (1) ....did you start.... (you / start) acting?

NICOLE: When I (2) .... (be) 12. I (3) .... (go) to a drama school, and one day I (4) .... (sit) in the classroom and Nigel Stewart, the famous film director, (5) .... (walk) in. He (6) .... (see) me, and that (7) .... (be) the beginning.

INTERVIEWER: What (8) .... (be) your first film?

NICOLE: 'Holiday Home' with Terry Veale, who (9) .... (be) now my husband! We (10) .... (make) the film in Spain. We (11) .... (be) very young when we met – 17 and 13.

INTERVIEWER: I know that Terry (12) .... (have) an accident in that film. How (13) .... (it / happen)?

NICOLE: Well, one day near the end of the filming we (14) .... (ride) horses and Terry's horse suddenly (15) .... (stop) and he (16) .... (fall) off. He (17) .... (break) his arm. Today, Terry and I often (18) .... (talk) about our first meeting.

INTERVIEWER: (19) .... (you / ride) nowadays?

NICOLE: No, I (20) .... (stop) when I (21) .... (move) to Los Angeles.

INTERVIEWER: I know you are very busy, but what (22) .... (you / do) in your free time?

NICOLE: Well, Terry (23) .... (like) swimming – he (24) .... (swim) for two hours every day. And I (25) .... (love) cooking. The dish I (26) .... (make) for lunch today is a new idea of mine.

INTERVIEWER: Great! Nicole, can I ask you some more questions, and can I also talk to Terry?

NICOLE: Yes, of course. He (27) .... (swim) in our pool at the moment. Let's go outside and enjoy the sun. Come on.

I have done
(present perfect)

36 Put the verbs in the present perfect, positive or negative.

1 MUM: Can I use the computer please?

     JESSICA: Sorry, I ..... *haven't finished* ..... my homework yet. (finish)

2 NED: Is Paul enjoying his holiday in Australia?

     VICTOR: I hope so, but his mother ....

from him. I think she's a bit worried. (hear)

3 HELEN: Can I borrow your 'Shrek' DVD?

     CATHERINE: Sorry, I .... it.

I don't know where it is. (lose)

4 LUCY: Let's go and buy our tickets for the 'Pets' concert.

     JO: Don't worry. I .... already ....

them. (buy)

5 JACK: Does your dad like his new car?

     ANNIE: Well, he .... it yet, because he hasn't sold the old one.

(get)

6 NINA: I've got my driving test next week.

     MICHAEL: How many times .... you .... it? (take)

     NINA: This is the third time.

7 ROSEMARY: Let's take your parents to that new restaurant.

Do they like Japanese food?

     LUKE: I don't know. They .... never

.... it. (try)

8 ROB: Are you going to Pat's party tonight?

     JOSEPH: I don't know. Who .... he .... ? (invite)

     ROB: All the usual people I think – and those girls he met in London.

9 JOHN: I enjoyed reading that new novel by Sarah Cunliffe. Is it her first book?

     LIZ: No, she .... three, but I think this is her best. (write)

10 FRAN: John looks thinner, doesn't he?

     ALISON: Yes. .... he .... weight? (lose)

11 IAN: Why doesn't this DVD player work?

     ROLAND: I think you .... it. (break)

12 NEIL: Where are my keys?

     SALLY: I don't know. I .... them. (see)

7 You work for a travel agency. Jack Brown, a customer, is interested in one of your walking holidays in the tropical rain forests of South America. You are asking him some questions. Complete the questions with **Have you ever ... ?**

	YOU	JACK
1	Can you walk a long distance? *Have you ever walked* (walk) more than 40 kilometres?	Yes, no problem. Yes, often.
2	Are you healthy? .... (have) a serious illness? .... (break) an arm or a leg?	Yes, very. No, never. My leg, twice.
3	Do you enjoy your food? .... (eat) crocodile?	Yes, very much. No, never.
4	Can you swim? .... (travel) in a canoe?	Yes. Yes, once.
5	Can you read a map? .... (lose) your way?	I think so. No, never.
6	Do you sleep well? .... (sleep) outside?	Yes, always. Yes, many times.
7	Are you afraid of heights? .... (climb) a high mountain?	No. Yes, once.

Now write three sentences about what Jack has done and two sentences about what he hasn't done.

Jack has done a lot of things in his life. *He has (often) walked more than 40 kilometres.*

He has never had a serious illness.

And what about you?

I've never walked more than 40 kilometres.

29

38　Write **has/have been** or **has/have gone**.

1　HARRY:　I saw you in Annabel's Restaurant last night.
　　DIANA:　No, it wasn't me. I ....'ve.... never ....been.... there.

2　SAM:　Roberto and Sophie are on holiday, aren't they? Where .... they .... ?
　　SUE:　To Florida, again.
　　SAM:　How many times .... they .... there?
　　SUE:　This is their third visit.

3　JOE:　Can I have an apple, please?
　　MARY:　We haven't got any. I .... n't .... to the shops today.

4　ALAN:　Where's Emma?
　　MARK:　She's got a headache, so she .... to bed.

5　STEVE:　*(on the phone)* Can I speak to Manuela, please?
　　KATH:　She's out, I'm afraid. She .... to the cinema.
　　STEVE:　Again? She .... already .... to the cinema three times this week.

39　Complete what James is saying using verbs in the present perfect.

James

JAMES:　See that man over there, Alice? I'm sure I (1) ....'ve seen.... him on TV. Oh yes, I
　　　　remember, it's David Sen – the man I'm going to see at the Festival Hall tonight. He's a
　　　　wonderful piano player. He and his family (2) .... a lot of different things
　　　　in their lives. He (3) .... all over the world, playing the piano, and he
　　　　(4) .... a lot of interesting people. He (5) .... a lot of money
　　　　in piano-playing competitions, so he's rich now. His daughter's only 20 and she
　　　　(6) .... already .... a very successful cookery book and
　　　　she's writing another one now. That's his son, Kenny, with him. He loves motorbikes. He
　　　　(7) .... his bike all the way from Canada to Chile, and he
　　　　(8) .... just .... the story of his journey to a travel
　　　　magazine. So he'll be rich soon! David Sen's wife is a musician too. She plays the flute.
　　　　They (9) .... together many times in different countries. But they
　　　　(10) .... never .... to this country before, so I'm going to
　　　　their concert at the Festival Hall tonight.

ALICE:　You certainly know a lot about him!

How long have you ... ?
(present perfect questions)

0 Read the information about Cheryl Atkins. Ask Cheryl some questions with **How long ... ?** + the present perfect simple. Then complete Cheryl's answers with **for** and **since**.

My name is Cheryl Atkins and (1) <u>I live in London</u>. (2) <u>I'm married to Paul</u> and we have a 1-year-old baby girl, Rita. (3) <u>We also have a new dog.</u> (4) <u>I work as a hairdresser.</u> (5) <u>Paul is a train driver.</u> (6) <u>My parents live with us</u> and (7) <u>my mother looks after the baby</u>. She also looks after my father. (8) <u>He is ill.</u>

	YOU		CHERYL
1	How long have you lived in London	?	Since 2002.
2		?	.... more than five years.
3		?	.... last week.
4		?	.... I left school.
5		?	.... about nine months.
6		?	.... a long time.
7		?	.... Rita was born.
8		?	.... the beginning of this year.

1 Complete the sentences with **for** (**for ten minutes** etc.), **since** (**since 5 o'clock** etc.) or **ago** (**two hours ago** etc.). Use your own ideas.

1 You can't be hungry. You had lunch <u>half an hour ago</u> .

2 Jane is fed up. Her friend is late. She's been waiting <u>for an hour / since 3 o'clock</u> .

3 I don't live in London now. I moved to Paris ....

4 I now live in Paris. I've been here ....

5 Tom's grandfather died ....

6 Maggie's got flu. She's been in bed ....

7 Sue and Richard got married .... and their first child was born ....

8 I like Mary's hair. She's had it in that style ....

What about you? Write your own short answers to these questions. Use **for**, **since** and **ago**.

9	How long have you lived in the place where you're living now?	....
10	When did you last play a sport?	....
11	How long have you had this book?	....
12	When did you start doing this exercise?	....
13	How long have you been a student?	....
14	When did you last buy a pair of shoes?	....
15	How long have you been able to speak English?	....

42 Complete the postcard with the present perfect simple, the present perfect continuous or the past simple.

We (1) ....**arrived**....... (arrive) here in Cape Town six days ago. I can't believe we (2) .... (be) here since last Sunday – we've done such a lot. At the moment we're waiting for a boat to take us on a trip round the harbour. But it's late. We (3) .... (wait) for about half an hour. David flew in 24 hours ago, but he (4) .... (be) in bed since he arrived. He's got a horrible cold – he (5) .... (have) it for a week. The weather is a bit strange – rain for five days, but today the sun is shining. It (6) .... (shine) since we got up this morning.

   Two days ago we (7) .... (go) to visit my aunt Nina – she (8) .... (live) here for more than 20 years. She (9) .... (get married) a year ago. She (10) .... (know) Alfie (that's his name) for years – so I've got a new uncle!
Hey great! The boat has arrived. Bye for now.

Kristen

43 Write a sentence for each situation. Use the present perfect continuous (has/have been doing etc.) + for/since.

1 Sam and I arranged to meet at the cinema at 7 o'clock. I arrived on time, but I'm still waiting for Sam to arrive.
   I ....have been waiting for Sam since 7 o'clock..

2 John started his phone call 20 minutes ago and he's still talking.
   John ....

3 Olga and Peter are tired. They started walking six hours ago and they're still walking.
   They ....

4 You started watching TV at 9 o'clock this morning and you're still watching it.
   You ....

5 Laura felt sick at lunchtime today and she's still feeling sick.
   Laura ....

6 Fred got on the Trans-Europe express train on the 28th of June. Today it's the 30th of June and he's still travelling.
   Fred ....

7 I hate this weather. It started raining 12 hours ago and it's still raining.
   It ....

I have done and I did
(present perfect and past simple)

4 Write questions. Use the present perfect or the past simple. Read the answers first.

1 How long / Sarah / live / in Poland?
  How long has Sarah lived in Poland ?
  Since 2000.

2 When / John / lose / his job?
  ?
  Three weeks ago.

3 How long / Ricardo / have / a cat?
  ?
  Since January.

4 What time / you / finish / work last night?
  ?
  At 9 o'clock.

5 When / last time / you / have / a holiday?
  ?
  Last year.

6 How long / you / watch / TV / last night?
  ?
  All evening.

7 When / Chris / go out?
  ?
  Ten minutes ago.

8 How long / your father / be / in hospital?
  ?
  Since Monday.

5 There are mistakes in eight of these sentences. Correct the sentences where necessary. Write 'OK' if the sentence is already correct.

1 When <u>have Tim and Annie been</u> to India?   When did Tim and Annie go to India?
2 I'm here since last year.
3 Maria has just written a book. It's very good.
4 Sue's an actor. She's been a photographer five years ago.
5 James and I have met last March.
6 The weather has been cold for many days.
7 John is looking for a new job since last month.
8 Have you spoken to your parents last night?
9 I played the guitar since I was a child.
10 What have you done last night?

33

46 Tick (✓) the best ending for each sentence.

1 I've already been to the museum,
A after I was in London.
B so I don't want to go again. ✓

2 David and Akemi have been married for five years
A and they were very happy.
B and they are very happy.

3 Maggie and Di met in 1988
A and started a business together two years later.
B and have started a business together two years later.

4 Jackie has been ill
A yesterday.
B all day.

5 I went to Italy
A in the summer.
B since my birthday.

6 John has gone out,
A so don't phone him.
B when he heard the news.

47 Complete the second sentence in each pair. Use the present perfect or the past simple.

1 How long have you been here?
When ...._did you arrive_........ ? (arrive)

2 When did Jane buy her computer?
How long .... ? (have)

3 Clare became a politician 20 years ago.
Clare .... 20 years. (be)

4 Joe started work here in 2004.
Joe .... since 2004. (work)

5 I am still doing my homework.
I .... yet. (finish)

6 Matt has known his best friend, Ahmed, for two years.
Matt first .... two years ago. (meet)

7 Adam and Sam have both got flu. It started a week ago.
Adam and Sam .... a week. (have)

8 Julia was first interested in music when she was five years old.
Julia .... since she was five. (be)

3 Put the verbs in the present perfect or the past simple.

'Here is the Six o'clock News from ITC, on Monday the 25th of April.

Our reporter in Nepal (1) .....*telephoned*..... (telephone) us ten minutes ago and (2) .....*said*..... (say) that Junko Shimoto and her partner, Miki Sato, are on top of the world today. They (3) .... (reach) the top of Mount Everest half an hour ago. Our reporter spoke to another climber on the expedition.

REPORTER: Are Junko and Miki still on the top of Mount Everest?

CLIMBER: No, they (4) .... (just start) their return journey.

REPORTER: How long (5) .... they .... (spend) up there?

CLIMBER: About ten minutes. They (6) .... (take) some photos of each other.

REPORTER: Are they in good health?

CLIMBER: Well, they're both tired, but they're fine.

The President of Volponia, Madame Fernoff, (7) .... (arrive) in Britain last night. Madame Fernoff (8) .... (be) President since 2001. She said she was happy to be in Britain.

At yesterday's meeting of European finance ministers, Jack Delaney, the Irish Finance Minister, (9) .... (say), 'I am going to leave my job soon. I (10) .... (work) very hard, and I want to spend more time with my family.' Mr Delaney (11) .... (be) Irish Finance Minister for five years.

Last night, Camford United (12) .... (win) the football league championship. The team (13) .... (win) the championship four times now – the first time (14) .... (be) in1986. In their final game yesterday, Bryan Riggs (15) .... (score) the winning goal. Riggs (16) .... (be) with the team since he (17) .... (leave) school.

And now to the weather. We (18) .... (have) a lot of rain over the country since the beginning of the week and unfortunately this will continue until the end of the weekend. For your information, last week (19) .... (be) the wettest April week for 100 years.

And that's the end of tonight's news.'

49   Put the verbs in the present perfect or the past simple.

1 CLARE: ....Have........ you ......seen...... John? (see)

   MARCUS: No, why?

   CLARE: He ....'s broken.... his leg. (break)

   MARCUS: Really? When ......did...... he ......do...... that? (do)

   CLARE: Yesterday.

2 ADAM: Oh no! I .... my wallet.
            I can't find it. (lose)

   TONY: When .... you last .... it? (see)

   ADAM: This morning when I .... the house. (leave)

3 MARY: Alan's going to sell his car.

   SIMON: Really? He only .... it last month. (buy)

   MARY: I know. He just loves changing cars.

   SIMON: How many cars .... he .... in his life? (have)

   MARY: At least 20.

4 BEN: Can I look at the newspaper, please?

   VAL: In a minute. I .... with it yet.
            (not / finish)

   BEN: You're very slow. You ....
            it this morning after breakfast. (start)

5 JULIA: There was a good programme on TV last night
            about elephants. .... you .... it? (see)

   SARAH: Yes, it was wonderful. .... you ever
            .... a LIVE elephant? (see)

   JULIA: Yes, and I .... one. (also touch)

   SARAH: When .... that? (be)

   JULIA: Two years ago when I ....
            on holiday in Kenya. (be)

6 PATRICK: Connie looks really fed up. What's the matter?

   DAN: She .... her car again. (crash)

   PATRICK: Again! How many times .... she .... that? (do)

   DAN: I think about four.

I do / I have done / I did
(present, present perfect and past)

0 Complete the questions.

MARCO: (1) ......*What's*...... your job?

PETE: I'm an engineer with National Telephones.

MARCO: How long (2) .... for that company?

PETE: About nine months.

MARCO: (3) .... it?

PETE: Not really. I preferred my old job.

MARCO: What (4) .... that?

PETE: I was a gardener.

TOM: Why (5) .... at me?

RUTH: Because you've got a bit of tomato on your face.

TOM: Where (6) .... it?

RUTH: On the right of your nose.

TOM: (7) .... or is it still there?

RUTH: It's still there.

1 Complete the letter. Use present, present perfect and past forms.

Hi Jo

Well, I (1) ......*arrived*...... (arrive) back safely two weeks ago. The flight (2) .... (be)
fine, but a bit long. I (3) .... (watch) two films and (4) .... (eat) two
breakfasts!

Thanks for everything. I (5) .... (have) a really good time with you in London. I hope
you (6) .... (enjoy) it too. Everything here is very different from London. I
(7) .... (write) this letter outside in the garden. I (8) .... (sit) under a
big umbrella because the sun is very hot today. I know we (9) .... (have) some sunny
days in London, but I remember there (10) .... (be) also some rain.

It was difficult for me to start work after my wonderful holiday, but it's OK now. I
(11) .... (be) in a new department since I (12) .... (come) home, and it's
interesting. I (13) .... (have) a new manager now, and that's good because the old one
(14) .... (be) horrible to me.

(15) .... (you / like) rock music? My brother (16) .... (practise) in
his room at the moment and it's quite loud! I (17) .... (just / send) you some of his CDs.
I hope you like them.

By the way, (18) .... (you / find) a black leather photo album? I think I
(19) .... (leave) it in the bedroom. Could you send it to me sometime? No hurry.

Jill (20) .... (sit) in the garden with me and she sends her love to you. Please write
or call soon, and thank you again for a wonderful time.

Love, Chris

52 Write Jo's reply. Use the words to write complete sentences.

Dear Chris

1 Thank you for your letter. Yes, I / enjoy / the time you / spend / with me very much. We / have / some good fun.

 <u>Thank you for your letter. Yes, I enjoyed the</u>

2 You / leave / a big box of chocolates for my parents. Thank you. We / just / finish / them – they / be delicious.

....

3 And thank you also for the CDs. They / arrive / yesterday. I / not / play / all of them yet. At the moment I / listen / to 'Paradise Rock'. It / be / very good.

....

4 My mother / find / your photo album the day you / leave. I / send / it back two weeks ago. you / receive / it yet?

....

5 Do you remember Steve? We / meet / him at Sue's party. Well, he / come / to my house last week. He / ask / for your address, so I / give / it to him. I hope that's OK. He / be / in California now on business.

....

6 I / look / out of the window at the moment. The sun / shine / and it / be / a beautiful warm day. In fact, it / be / sunny every day since you / go back / to San Francisco. Honestly!

....

7 The CD / just / finish. Tell your brother I love his music. he / want / a publicity agent in London?

....

That's all for now.
Lots of love,
Jo

Last week you stayed with a friend for a few days, but now you're home again. Write a 'thank you' letter to your friend. Use the following ideas and the letter from Chris to Jo to help you.

- Thank your friend.
- Write about the journey home.
- Write about the things you enjoyed when you were with your friend.
- You are sending a present – tell him/her about it.
- Write about what you're doing now.
- Ask your friend to write to you.

is done / was done and is being done / has been done
(passive)

3 Complete the crossword with the past participles.

Down	Across
1 choose	5 read
2 write	6 buy
3 make	8 grow
4 find	9 speak
7 think	10 forget
10 feel	12 hold
11 shoot	13 take
	14 build

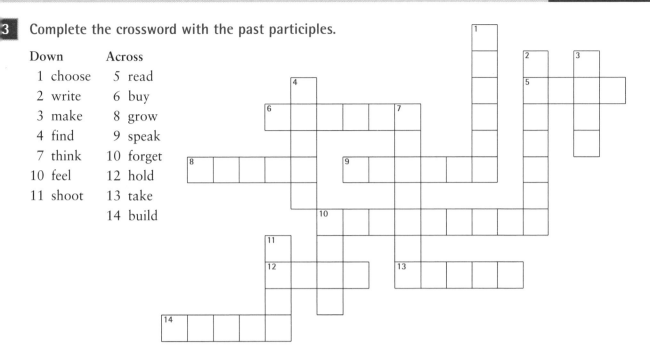

4 Use some of the past participles from the crossword to write questions. For questions 1–4, use the present passive; for questions 5–9, use the past passive. What are the right answers? You can check at the bottom of the page.

1 In which continent / tigers / find?
   In which continent are tigers found .... ? A Africa   B Asia

2 How many languages / speak / in the world?
   .... ? A about 500   B about 5,000

3 Where / coffee / grow?
   .... ? A Kenya   B France

4 What / the country of Siam / now call?
   .... ? A China   B Thailand

5 When / 'Romeo and Juliet' / write?
   When was 'Romeo and Juliet' written .... ? A in the 1590s   B in the 1740s

6 When / first photograph / take?
   .... ? A 1827   B 1893

7 Where / CDs / first make?
   .... ? A China   B the Netherlands

8 When / Taj Mahal / build?
   .... ? A 1631   B 1931

9 Where / John Lennon / shoot?
   .... ? A New York   B Liverpool

1B   2B   3A   4B   5A   6A   7B   8A   9A

Answers

55 Look at the picture of Hartson's jam factory. A visitor is being shown around the factory by the manager. Complete what he says. Use the present simple or present continuous passive.

The machines (1) ___are switched on___ (switch on) at 7.30 every morning and they (2) ___are turned off___ (turn off) at 5.30. The factory (3) .... (lock) at 6.30 by our security guards and all the staff (4) .... (check) before they go home. We don't want our jam to disappear! Now as you can see, strawberry jam (5) .... (make) here today. And over there the jars of jam (6) .... (put) into boxes by our team. Hartson's jam (7) .... (not/export) because this country buys everything we produce. It's very important to keep our factory clean and hygienic, so everything (8) .... (wash) very carefully every night. Of course nobody (9) .... (allow) to smoke anywhere in the factory. Now I think lunch (10) .... (serve) in the canteen at the moment, so shall we go?

56 Look at the pictures. What has been done and what hasn't been done since 4.30? Write sentences.

what has been done
The flowers have been thrown away.
....
....
....
....

what hasn't been done
The cups haven't been washed.
....
....
....

7   Put the verbs in the correct form, active or passive.

STUDIO: Here is the local news for today, Friday the 23rd of November. Last night in Cowford, many trees (1) ......*were blown*...... (blow) down in the storm. One tree (2) ...*fell*... (fall) across the main road into Cowford. It damaged the telephone lines. The tree (3) .... (take) away by the fire service during the night. Heavy rain also (4) .... (cause) problems on the roads. Some roads (5) .... (cover) by half a metre of water. Many motorists (6) .... (leave) their cars and (7) .... (walk) home. Now, over to our reporter, Carol Black.

CAROL: The situation this morning is better and nearly back to normal. I can see the telephone engineers at work. The broken lines (8) .... (repair) at the moment, so people will soon be able to use their phones again. There is no water on the roads – it (9) .... (disappear). And the last few cars (10) .... just .... (remove) by the emergency services.

STUDIO: Thank you, Carol. And some football news. We (11) .... just .... (hear) that Cowford Town are the champions for the fourth time. A few minutes ago the referee (12) .... (blow) his whistle at the end of the game against Grimetown United. Our reporter at the match, Kevin Anderton, (13) .... (wait) to talk to us at the stadium. Kevin, (14) .... it a good game?

KEVIN: Yes, excellent, but unfortunately a bit rough. Cowford's star player, Tony Ancock, (15) .... (send) off because he (16) .... (kick) one of the Grimetown players. And the Grimetown goalkeeper (17) .... (hurt) when he (18) .... (crash) into one of the goalposts. He (19) .... (carry) off the field with leg injuries, so both teams (20) .... (play) with ten men for the last few minutes.

STUDIO: Is he all right?

KEVIN: Well, we don't know. He (21) .... (take) to hospital right now. The manager (22) .... (think) it's serious.

STUDIO: Oh dear. That's a bad end for Grimetown. What (23) .... (happen) now in the stadium?

KEVIN: The Cowford players (24) .... (give) the Champions Cup. And now back to the studio.

Write a short report of something that has happened for your local TV news. Use one of these ideas to help you.

Bank robbery: €6 million taken	Dog attacks man outside supermarket
Local woman wins lottery	Car hits actor on bike

....

....

....

58 Complete the sentences with the correct form of **be**, **have** and **do**. Use positive and negative verbs.

1 I ......*am*...... reading the newspaper at the moment.
2 Frank isn't at work at the moment. He .... gone to Switzerland for a conference.
3 The Channel Tunnel .... built between 1985 and 1994.
4 Philip .... eat meat. He's a vegetarian.
5 We .... been to Toronto before. This is our first time in Canada.
6 Look! How strange! Our cat .... playing with the dog from next door.
7 Your jeans .... washed last week and now they're dirty again.
8 I turned the music off because you .... listening to it.
9 A lot of leather shoes .... imported from Italy every year.
10 I was tired, so I .... go out last night.

59 Complete the sentences with the past simple (**sold**, **broke** etc.) or the past participle (**rung**, **gone** etc.).

1 Sue ......*sold*...... (sell) her motorbike when she ......*broke*...... (break) her leg last year.
2 I've ......*rung*...... (ring) the doorbell three times and there's no answer. I think they've ......*gone*...... (go) out.
3 I .... (give) the letter to Ruth, but she .... (forget) to post it.
4 Ian hasn't .... (find) his credit cards yet. He can't remember where he .... (leave) them.
5 Do you remember the photo of Don that you .... (show) me? Was it .... (take) by a professional photographer?
6 A lion .... (escape) from the national zoo yesterday, but it was .... (catch) a few hours later.
7 James has often .... (think) about learning to fly, but he hasn't .... (do) it yet.
8 When she was younger, Pat always .... (wear) a ring which was .... (give) to her by her grandmother.
9 Alan .... (learn) to swim when he was a baby. But he .... (fall) into a river when he was four years old and he's never .... (swim) again.
10 Jill .... (feel) ill last night, so she .... (go) to bed and .... (sleep) for ten hours.

Complete the questions that you ask about a friend's new camera.

YOU

1 You've already got a good camera, so why ....*did you*.... buy a new one?
2 How long .... had it?
3 .... get it in a shop or on-line?
4 .... very expensive?
5 Why .... choose that model?
6 .... learnt how to use it yet?
7 Where .... made?
8 .... take good pictures?
9 .... usually put your photos on your computer?
10 Your husband likes cameras. .... tried your new camera yet?

Now complete what your friend says. Use the past simple or the past participle.

'I (11) ....*broke*.... (break) my old camera a few months ago, so I (12) .... (buy) this
new one. I've only (13) .... (have) it for two weeks. I (14) .... (get) it
on-line and it wasn't very expensive. I (15) .... (choose) this model because I
(16) .... (read) about it in a photography magazine. It was (17) ....
(make) in Japan. I've (18) .... (learn) how to use it, but I'm not very good yet. I
(19) .... (take) some
pictures last week and they were
brilliant. I (20) ....
(put) my first lot of pictures on my
computer last weekend and I've just
(21) .... (send) them to
my sister. And no, nobody else has
(22) .... (use) the
camera yet, but I've
(23) .... (show) Bill
how it works.'

61 Josie Turner is the export manager of a large international company. Harry Brentwood is a customer from Canada. They are trying to arrange an appointment for next week. Look at their diaries and complete the conversation. Use the present continuous (**'s coming** etc.) or the present simple (**comes** etc.).

JOSIE: Hello, Josie Turner speaking.

HARRY: Oh Josie, this is Harry Brentwood. How are you? I (1) ....'m coming.... to London on Sunday and I'd like to meet you next week. Can we arrange a time?

JOSIE: Sure. When are you free?

HARRY: Well, how about lunch on Monday?

JOSIE: I can't, I'm afraid. I (2) .... lunch with our new chairman. How about Tuesday at 10.30?

HARRY: No, no good. Dennis, my London agent, (3) .... to the office on Tuesday morning. Wednesday afternoon is a possibility.

JOSIE: Not for me. My secretary, Jenny, (4) .... and all of us from the office
(5) .... to the wedding. And on Thursday morning I
(6) .... to Manchester for a meeting with Bill Syms.

HARRY: What time (7) .... the meeting .... ?

JOSIE: At 11.30. I've got an idea. Why don't you come with me? We can talk on the way.

HARRY: That sounds good. Oh, but wait a minute, I can't. I
(8) .... to some people about business opportunities in Canada at lunchtime.

JOSIE: So Friday, then?

HARRY: Yes, that's the only possibility because my return flight to Montreal (9) .... early on Saturday morning. So, how about 11.30 on Friday morning at your office?

JOSIE: Yes, that's perfect. Looking forward to seeing you then.

2 Some friends of yours invite you to do different things next week, but you can't do any of them because you're busy. Write what you're doing at those times. Use the present continuous (**I'm having** etc.).

YOUR FRIEND   *YOU*

1 There's a party at my house on Tuesday night. Would you like to come?

I can't, I'm afraid. *I'm having dinner with Mary.*

2 Meet me on Wednesday evening in the city centre.

I can't, I'm afraid.

3 See you on Friday at 1 o'clock outside the museum. OK?

I can't, I'm afraid.

4 Jim wants you to come to the cinema with us on Saturday afternoon.

I can't, I'm afraid.

5 Let's go for a walk on Sunday.

I can't, I'm afraid.

3 Marta and her friends, Emma and Jane, are going on holiday tomorrow to China. Marta is emailing Emma with lots of questions. Write Marta's questions. Use the present simple or the present continuous.

1 What time / the flight / leave?   *What time does the flight leave*   ?
2 What time / we / meet / tomorrow?   *What time are we meeting tomorrow*   ?
3 When / the check-in desk / open?   ?
4 How / we / travel / to the airport?   ?
5 Where / we / meet / Jane?   ?
6 Where / we / stay / for the first night?   ?
7 What time / flight / land?   ?
8 Who / meet / us / at the airport in Beijing?   ?

Now use your own ideas to write Emma's answers.

The flight leaves at 9 o'clock in the evening. We're meeting at

45

64   Write questions with **going to**.

1   BEN: What / Dad / do?
      What's Dad going to do   ?
  MUM: Paint the kitchen walls.
  BEN: What colour / he / do them?
      What colour's he going to do them   ?
  MUM: White.

2   JILL: What / you / buy / for Paul's birthday?
                                  ?
  MEG: I don't know yet.
  JILL: he / have / a party?
                                    ?
  MEG: Yes, on Saturday.

3   TIM: you / buy / a new computer?
                                    ?
  SAM: Yes.
  TIM: What kind / you / get?
                                    ?
  SAM: A Bell laptop, I think.

4   MARY: What / Sarah / do / after university?
                                    ?
  JACK: First, she's going to travel.
  MARY: How long / she / be away?
                                    ?
  JACK: About six months.

5   SALLY: Chris and Kate / get married?
                                    ?
  PAUL: Yes, it's great news, isn't it?
  SALLY: Where / they / live?
                                    ?
  PAUL: With her parents.

5 What are you, and your friends and family **going to do** or **not going to do** this evening? Use these ideas to write sentences about yourself, and your friends and family.

read a book	cook dinner	listen to music	spend a lot of money
email a friend	wash (your) hair	play on the computer	watch TV
clean (your) room	do some work	eat some chocolate	phone a friend

I'm not going to read a book this evening.
My mother is going to cook dinner.
....
....
....
....

6 Complete the sentences. Use **going to.**

1 It's only 7 o'clock in the morning, but the sun is shining and it's warm.
   It *'s going to be* a beautiful day.
2 John is driving on the wrong side of the road!
   He .... an accident!
3 Eve is eating her third box of chocolates!
   .... sick!
4 What a fantastic race! Roger's nearly there! Only 50 metres to the finish.
   .... win!
5 Look at those boys on that big bicycle! They're not safe.
   .... fall off!
6 This film is making me feel very sad.
   .... cry.

47

67 Read what George says about his life at the moment and his future.

At the moment, I have to work very hard. I study at home every night. It's Friday today, but I'll be at home as usual this evening. I'll be in my bedroom with my books.

But tomorrow is Saturday – no college and no work! So tomorrow morning, I'll probably be in the city centre. I want to buy some clothes.

College finishes next month, so at the end of the month I'll be on holiday in Paris with my friends.

A few years from now, I'll probably be married. In 2030, I'll be 40 years old. My children will probably be at school. I don't know where I'll be in 2050.

Now correct the sentences that are not true. Use **will** and **won't**.

1 George will be at the cinema this evening. ⸺ No, he won't. He'll be at home.
2 He'll be in his bedroom. ⸺ True.
3 Tomorrow morning, he'll be at college. ⸺
4 Next month, he'll be in Paris. ⸺
5 He'll be on holiday on his own. ⸺
6 A few years from now, he'll probably be married. ⸺
7 He'll be 30 in 2030. ⸺
8 His children will probably be at university in 2030. ⸺
9 He'll be in Paris in 2050. ⸺

 And what about you? Where will you be? Write sentences about yourself. Use **I'll be / I'll probably be / I don't know where I'll be**.

This evening ⸺
Tomorrow morning ⸺
Next month ⸺
A few years from now ⸺
In 2030 ⸺

8   What do you say in these situations? Write two sentences for each situation. Use **I think I'll /
he'll** etc. and **I don't think they'll / she'll** etc.

1   Your favourite baseball team, the Milton Reds, are playing very well at the moment. The last
    time they were beaten was two years ago. They have a match on Saturday.
    I think .... *the Milton Reds will win the match.* ....
    I don't think .... *they will lose.* ....

2   You have to go out tonight, but you've hurt your foot so it's difficult to walk. You could go by
    car.
    I don't think ....
    I think ....

3   Your brother has got a history exam tomorrow. He likes history and he's done a lot of work.
    I don't think ....
    I think ....

4   Your grandparents don't like the cold winters in Scotland. They want to move to a warm
    country. They're thinking about Australia.
    I think ....
    I don't think ....

5   Kim doesn't like her job at the garage. She's been talking about changing jobs for a long time,
    but she's still at the garage.
    I think ....
    I don't think ....

6   Jana wants to sell her old computer and buy a new one. The problem is she doesn't have enough
    money for a new one.
    I don't think ....
    I think ....

69 Carol's grandmother has a few problems, so Carol offers to help her. Write sentences with **Shall I ... ?**

1	Oh dear! I can't read Jane's letter.	*Shall I read* .... it to you?
2	I'm thirsty.	.... you a cup of tea?
3	It's a bit cold in here.	.... the window?
4	I can't open this packet of biscuits.	.... it for you?
5	I can't hear the TV.	.... it up?
6	The dog needs some exercise.	.... him for a walk?
7	I think the kitchen floor is dirty.	.... it for you?

70 Joe and Phil went camping in Portugal last year. Now they're planning their next holiday. Write questions with **Shall we ... ?** Read the answers first, then write the questions.

JOE: It's time to start planning this summer's holiday. Where
(1) ...... *shall we go* ...... ?

PHIL: Let's go to Portugal again. I enjoyed it last year.

JOE: (2) .... in the same
hotel?

PHIL: No, let's try something different. How about camping?

JOE: Great! I bought a new tent last month.

(3) .... that?

PHIL: Yes, good idea. (4) ....
or fly?

JOE: Oh, drive I think because we'll have a lot of luggage.

PHIL: When (5) .... ?

JOE: The middle of July is best for me. How about you?

PHIL: July's fine with me too.

(6) .... Tony to come
with us?

JOE: No. The tent is only big enough for two people!

I am doing / I am going to do / I'll do
(future forms)

1 Which is right?

> Hi Mark
>
> I know (1) <u>you're working</u> / ~~you'll work~~ in Sweden in June, but what (2) <u>are you doing</u> / <u>do you do</u> for the first two weeks in July? Hannah and I (3) <u>are going</u> / <u>will go</u> to the Czech Republic for a holiday, and we want you and Sue to come with us! I don't think Hannah (4) <u>will fly</u> / <u>flies</u> to the Czech Republic because she hates planes, so (5) <u>are we going</u> / <u>shall we go</u> by train? What do you think?
>
> We can spend a few days in Prague and then go to the mountain area and do some walking. (6) <u>We're not going to camp</u> / <u>We won't camp</u> this year. I think (7) <u>we'll probably stay</u> / <u>we're probably staying</u> in small hotels.
>
> Good plans? Anyway, Hannah's calling me. (8) <u>We're going to have</u> / <u>We will have</u> dinner, but (9) <u>I'll phone</u> / <u>I'm phoning</u> you later this evening.
>
> Jack

2 Write complete sentences.

1 present continuous or *will*?

JIM: everybody / come / to the meeting on Friday afternoon?
  <u>Is everybody coming to the meeting on Friday afternoon?</u>

PAM: Most people.

JIM: it / be / a long meeting? <u>Will it be a long meeting?</u>

PAM: I'm not sure. It / probably / be /about three hours. Why?

JIM: I / go / to the dentist at 5.30. I made the appointment two weeks ago.

2 present simple or *going to*?

TOM: Great! That's the end of school for a few weeks.

LUCY: When / the next term / begin?

TOM: On the 3rd of September.

LUCY: What / you / do / during the holidays?

TOM: I don't know yet. What about you?

LUCY: My school / not / finish / until next week.
  Then I / look / for a job for the summer.

3 *will* or *going to*?

VAL: Do you want to play tennis on Friday?

BEN: I can't. I / visit my grandmother.

VAL: Does she live near?

BEN: Not really. About 100 kilometres away. I usually drive, but my car isn't working at the moment. I / take / it to the garage tomorrow.

VAL: I / lend / you mine. I don't need it on Friday.

BEN: Oh thanks a lot. I / pay for / the petrol.

51

73 Are these sentences OK? Correct the verbs that are wrong.

1 The new road <u>shall</u> be open in the summer.   *will*

2 The exam <u>starts</u> at 9.00 tomorrow.   *OK*

3 I've got an appointment. I <u>will see</u> the dentist
   tomorrow.

4 Come in, Joe. You look cold. Sit down.
   <u>I'm making</u> you a cup of tea.

5 What time <u>is</u> the sun <u>rising</u> tomorrow?

6 Where <u>do</u> you <u>go</u> for lunch tomorrow?

7 <u>Shall</u> we <u>learn</u> Spanish next year?

8 Do you think it <u>is snowing</u> later?

9 I can't come because <u>I'll be</u> on holiday.

10 *(on the phone)* You need to speak to Ann.
   Just a moment, please. <u>I'm going to call</u> her.

11 Don't worry about me, Mum. <u>I'll email</u> you
   every day from New Zealand.

74 What do you say in the following situations? Use **will** (**will go/do** etc.) or the present continuous (**am going / is doing** etc.).

1 Jane tells you she cannot play tennis tonight because her partner is ill. You offer to play with
   her. What do you say?
   I'll play with you.

2 Your young brother has broken his favourite toy train. He's very sad. You offer to buy him
   another one. What do you say?

3 You and your sister have arranged to go shopping tomorrow. A friend invites you to lunch.
   What do you say?
   I can't come, I'm afraid.

4 You're flying to Athens this afternoon. Your mother wants to know that you have arrived safely.
   You offer to telephone her this evening. What do you say?

5 Your brother, Tony, and his wife, Rachel, come to dinner once a week at your house. Tonight is
   the night. What do you say to your mother?
   Don't forget that   .

6 Franco wants to go to the cinema to see 'Black Nights'. It's a horror film and you know he
   doesn't like horror films. What do you say to him?
   I don't think   .

7 Julia wants to know about your weekend plans. What does she ask you?
                                                                        at the weekend?

8 You've arranged to go to the seaside for the weekend. What do you say to Julia?
                                                                        for the weekend.

52

5 Your friends are asking you about some plans. Complete your answers with **might (not)**.

1 JOE: Where are you going this weekend?
YOU: I don't know yet. __I might go to Tim's party__ (Tim's party), but __I might not go anywhere__ (not / anywhere).

2 PAUL: It's a national holiday tomorrow, so there's no public transport. How are Jane and Sue going to get here?
YOU: I don't know. They _____ (taxi), but _____ (not / come).

3 HELEN: Who are you going to invite for dinner?
YOU: I haven't decided yet. _____ (Sarah), but _____ (not / Tony).

4 SARAH: What new clothes does Clare want to buy on Saturday?
YOU: She's not sure yet. _____ (some jeans), but _____ (not / anything).

6 Your friend, Peter, is going on holiday tomorrow to China. Read the list of things he **is (not) going to** do and the things he **might (not)** do. Complete the email you send to another friend, Karen.

sure
1 visit the Forbidden City, Beijing
3 walk along the Great Wall
5 not eat western food
7 learn a little Chinese

perhaps
2 not have time to visit the museums
4 go on a boat trip down the Yangtse River
6 try green tea
8 not come home!

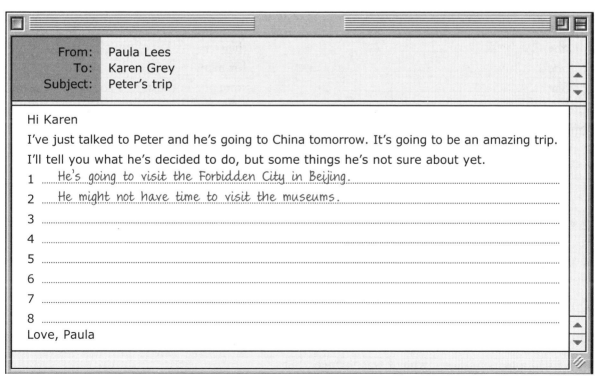

From: Paula Lees
To: Karen Grey
Subject: Peter's trip

Hi Karen
I've just talked to Peter and he's going to China tomorrow. It's going to be an amazing trip.
I'll tell you what he's decided to do, but some things he's not sure about yet.
1 __He's going to visit the Forbidden City in Beijing.__
2 __He might not have time to visit the museums.__
3 _____
4 _____
5 _____
6 _____
7 _____
8 _____
Love, Paula

77 Pat has got a problem. Complete what she says with **can** or **can't**.

'Oh dear! Where's my key? I (1) .....*can't*..... find it. Oh look! It's on the kitchen table. I (2) ....
see it. Now what am I going to do? I (3) .... get in. I (4) .... climb the tree to the
window on the first floor. It's too high. I (5) .... phone for help because I haven't got my
mobile with me. Hey, what's that noise in the sitting room? I (6) .... hear something. Oh
good, it's Peter. He's at home. Brilliant!'

The next day, Peter tells his friend, Kate, about Pat's problem. Complete the sentences.

7 Pat ....*couldn't find her key*.. yesterday.
8 She .... it on the kitchen table.
9 She .... in.
10 She .... the tree.
11 She .... for help.
12 She .... someone in the sitting room – it was me!

78 Complete the sentences. Use **can't** or **couldn't** and the verbs from the box.

| ~~answer~~ catch come cook ~~find~~ play see sleep understand |

1 I'd like to read Andrea's letter. The only problem is I .....*can't find*..... my glasses.
2 Lisa didn't pass her maths exam because she .....*couldn't answer*..... the questions.
3 I'd like to invite my friends to dinner at my house, but unfortunately I ....
4 Kevin was really tired last night, but he ....
5 People said he was a very interesting speaker, but I .... him.
6 I've got two tickets for the theatre on Saturday, but unfortunately Frank
....
7 Maria's dog ran out of the house and she .... it.
8 We had a piano at home when I was younger, but I .... it.
9 (*at the cinema*) Those people in front of me are very tall. I .... the screen.

9 Look at the information about Fred. Complete the sentences about him. Use **can/can't** or **could/couldn't**.

> Fred's mother is English and his father is German. When Fred was young:
>
>   ✓   ✗
>
> 1 understand German   speak it
> 2 play the guitar   sing
> 3 swim really well   ride a bike
> And now:
> 4 speak three languages fluently   play the guitar
> 5 play the piano   drive a car

1 When Fred was young, _he could understand German_ , but _he couldn't speak it_ .
2 He .... , but ....
3 .... , but ....
4 Now, Fred _can speak three languages fluently_ , but ....
5 .... , but ....

What about you? What could (or couldn't) you do when you were younger? What can (or can't) you do now? Write sentences with could/couldn't and can/can't. You can use the verbs from the box or think of your own ideas.

cook	drive	eat	make	play	run	sleep	speak	swim	understand	use

When I was younger, ...

....

Now, I ....

10 You're staying in a hotel. What do you say in these situations? Use **Could you ... ?** or **Could I ... ?**

1 You want the receptionist to turn the air-conditioning off in your room because you're cold.
   Could you turn the air-conditioning off, please?

2 There is only one towel in your room. You want another one.
   Could I have another towel, please?

3 There's no hair dryer in your room. You want to borrow one.
   ....

4 You want the receptionist to give you a wake-up call at 6.30 in the morning.
   ....

5 You want breakfast in your room tomorrow morning.
   ....

6 You want to leave your passport and traveller's cheques in the hotel safe.
   ....

7 You want the receptionist to get a taxi for you.
   ....

81 Complete one sentence with **must**, one sentence with **mustn't**, and one sentence with **don't/doesn't need to**.

1 Your friend Paul is going on holiday tomorrow. What do you say to him?

     *not necessary*

...You must buy... some suncream.
...You mustn't be... late for the flight.
...You don't need to take... your laptop because you aren't going to work on holiday.

2 Your parents are going away for the weekend. What do they say to you before they leave?

     *not necessary*

You .... for your exam next week.
You .... too much TV.
You .... There's plenty of food in the fridge.

3 You're ill in bed. Your friend comes to visit you. What does (s)he say?

   *not necessary*

You ....
You ....
You .... if you don't want to.

What about you? Write two things you **must(n't)** do in the next few days and two things you **don't need to** do. Explain why.

...I must buy a present for Anna because it's her birthday on Saturday.
....
....
....

82 Use your own ideas to complete the sentences. Use **must** or **had to**.

1 I've just heard Simon and Cara are getting married, so I ...must ring Sally and tell her... .
2 Unfortunately, my car didn't start yesterday, so I ...had to walk to my office... .
3 John had an important job to finish at the office last night, so he ....
4 The party finished late last night. So, if you're tired, you ....
5 Jamie forgot his front door key last night, so he ....
6 Alex had terrible toothache yesterday, so he ....
7 Come on! Our train leaves in an hour. We ....

3 Complete one sentence with **should** and one sentence with **shouldn't**.

1 GARY: I always feel tired these days. What do you think I should do?
  ANNE: ....*You should have*........ a holiday. ....*You shouldn't work*........ so hard.

2 GARY: I've got a hole in one of my teeth. What do you think I should do?
  ANNE: .... to the dentist.
          .... so many sweets.

3 GARY: I've got a terrible headache again. What do you think I should do?
  ANNE: .... an aspirin.
          .... without your glasses.

4 GARY: Bruno wants to borrow my car for the weekend, but he's a terrible driver. What do
          you think I should do?
  ANNE: .... him you need it.
          .... it to him.

4 You are asking a friend for advice. Write questions with **Do you think I/we should ... ?**

1 There are two buttons missing on this shirt I've just bought.
  ....*Do you think I should take*........ it back to the shop?

2 I think I work very hard, but I don't get a big salary.
  .... my boss for more money?

3 Jane is very nervous about going on holiday alone.
  .... with her?

4 Burnt toast again! This toaster is getting worse.
  .... a new one?

5 What advice would you give in the following situations? Use **should**.

1 Alan had a terrible argument with his wife at the weekend. It was his fault. What do you think
  he should do?
  I think ....*he should apologise to his wife.*........
  I don't think ....*she should speak to him until he apologises.*........

2 Maria has got some important exams. She's been invited to a party on Saturday night. What do
  you think she should do?
  I think ....
  I don't think ....

3 Joe is very intelligent, but he wants to leave school and get a job. His parents think he ought to
  go to university. What do you think he should do?
  I think ....
  I don't think ....

4 Dave and Rita haven't got much money, but they go out every night. At the end of the month
  they can't pay their electricity bills. What advice would you give?
  I think ....
  I don't think ....

86 Complete the sentences with the correct form of **have to**. Some of the sentences are in the present and some of them are in the past.

1 MARK: I don't like beans.
  SUE: That's OK. You _don't have to eat them_ . (eat)

2 DAVE: I have to write a 1,000-word story before next Friday.
  JILL: What about me? .... one too? (write)

3 ANN: CAN YOU PASS ME THE SALT, PLEASE?
  PETE: You .... ! I'm not deaf! (shout)

4 JOHN: Which job did Jenny accept?
  RUTH: She hasn't decided. She's going to think about it at the weekend. She
    .... yesterday. (choose)

5 GINA: What's the matter with Marcus today?
  TONY: I'm not sure. The doctor says he .... in
    bed for a few days. (stay)

6 JOE: Was Tina angry when you told her the news?
  MARK: She already knew it, so I .... her. (tell)

87 Beth and her grandmother are talking about school. Complete their conversation using the correct form of **have to**. Sometimes you need the present and sometimes the past. Read the conversation before you write.

GRAN: (1) _Do you have to go_ (go) to school tomorrow, Beth?
BETH: No, thank goodness. We've got a day off, but I have lots of
  homework to do.
  (2) .... (do) homework
  every night when you were at school?
GRAN: No, we didn't. School was easier in my time. But my school
  was a long way from my house – and we didn't have a car.
BETH: (3) How far .... (travel)?
GRAN: About five kilometres, twice a day. And you're lucky. At your school, you
  (4) .... (wear) uniform. We did, and I hated mine.
BETH: What colour was it?
GRAN: Red and grey, and I remember we (5) .... (wear) white
  gloves as well. Anyway, where's your brother at the moment?
BETH: In his room. He's got lots of exams next week, so he
  (6) .... (work) really hard.
GRAN: How many exams (7) .... (take)?
BETH: Seven or eight, I think. He (8) .... (get) good marks in
  them all if he wants to go to university.
GRAN: I finished school when I was 14 and (9) .... (do) any
  exams at all. Only the students who wanted to go to college
  (10) .... (take) exams.
BETH: So, school was easier in your day.
GRAN: Mmm, maybe.

Do this!   Don't do that!   Let's do this!

Unit 35

8 Read the email from Sally to her friend, Marie. Then complete the Rules of the House. Some sentences are positive (**go/turn** etc.) and some are negative (**don't go / don't come** etc.).

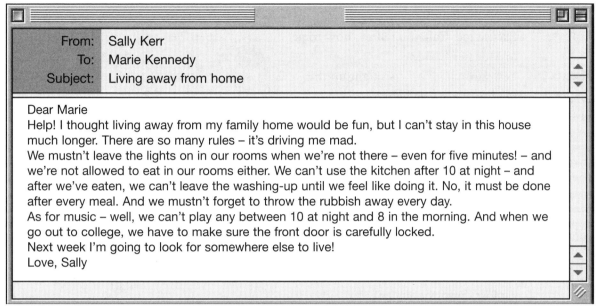

From: Sally Kerr
To: Marie Kennedy
Subject: Living away from home

Dear Marie
Help! I thought living away from my family home would be fun, but I can't stay in this house much longer. There are so many rules – it's driving me mad.
We mustn't leave the lights on in our rooms when we're not there – even for five minutes! – and we're not allowed to eat in our rooms either. We can't use the kitchen after 10 at night – and after we've eaten, we can't leave the washing-up until we feel like doing it. No, it must be done after every meal. And we mustn't forget to throw the rubbish away every day.
As for music – well, we can't play any between 10 at night and 8 in the morning. And when we go out to college, we have to make sure the front door is carefully locked.
Next week I'm going to look for somewhere else to live!
Love, Sally

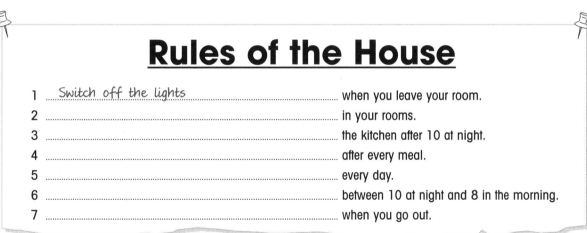

Rules of the House

1 _Switch off the lights_ .... when you leave your room.
2 .... in your rooms.
3 .... the kitchen after 10 at night.
4 .... after every meal.
5 .... every day.
6 .... between 10 at night and 8 in the morning.
7 .... when you go out.

What about you? What rules would you write for people living in your house? Think of two positive sentences and two negative sentences.

Rules of the House

....
....
....
....
....

89 Look at the map and complete the directions. Use the verbs from the box.

ask	cross	~~go~~	take	turn	walk

TOURIST: Excuse me. Can you tell me how to get to Munster Road?

LOCAL: Yes, sure. (1) ..Go.. straight up this road to the traffic lights. (2) .... right at the traffic lights. (3) .... along that road – I think it's called Craven Road – for about 100 metres. (4) .... the road – there's a pedestrian crossing there which is good because the road is really busy. (5) .... the second road on the left and that's Munster Road. (6) .... someone if you get lost, but it's quite easy to find.

Look at the map again. Give directions.

TOURIST: Excuse me. Can you tell me how to get to the supermarket?

LOCAL: ....
....
....
....

90 Write what you would say in these situations? Use imperatives (**have / go / don't go** etc.) or **Let's (not) / Don't let's**.

1 What do you say to someone just before they go out for the evening?
....Have a nice.... evening.

2 What do you say to a child who is opening the sitting room window?
.... the window. It's cold in here.

3 You've got a delicious chocolate cake. You want to offer your friend a piece. What do you say?
.... cake.

4 Your friend says, 'Shall we have take-away pizza tonight?' You want to go to the new Spanish restaurant for dinner. What do you say?
.... pizza. .... Spanish restaurant.

5 You have a headache and your brother is playing music very loudly. What do you say?
.... , please.

6 Your friend keeps asking you some questions about your job. You can't answer because it's a difficult situation at work at the moment. What do you say?
.... because I can't answer them.

60

I used to

91 George Medley is listening to a guide telling a group of visitors about the town of Stanton. He's thinking about Stanton in the past. Complete the sentences. Use **used to** and a suitable verb.

GUIDE

Stanton is a very busy town nowadays.
There are lots of things to do here.
For example, we have a new cinema complex.
And this is the chemical factory. It's very important. A lot of people work here.
Unfortunately, the river is not very clean now.
Pitt Street is the main shopping street in town.

We now have a wonderful city bus service.

And of course, we've got lots of fast food restaurants.
And look, there's Paul Carr, our famous artist.
As you can see, Stanton is a good place to live.

GEORGE

→ (1) ....It used to be........ very quiet.

→ (2) It .... a school.
→ (3) I ....
   football in the park there.
→ (4) I .... in that river.
→ (5) Our family .... in
   Pitt Street.
→ (6) Everyone ....
   to the shops.
→ (7) We ....
   at home.
→ (8) He .... in a bookshop.
→ (9) It .... better.

 Can you think of four things you used to do when you were younger that you don't do now? You can use the verbs from the box or think of your own ideas.

go	like	listen	live	play	speak

....

....

....

....

92 Complete the text about the Inuit people of North America. Use **used to** or the present simple form of the verbs from the box.

be ~~call~~ cook go hate hunt live ride spend take take off wear wear

IGLOO

FUR

SNOWSHOES

SEAL

The lives of the Inuit people of North America have changed a lot in 30 years. First, their name: people (1) ...... _used to call_ them Eskimos, but now they are called Inuits, which means 'the people'.

They (2) .... in igloos in the winter, but today, many of them live in houses in small towns. They (3) .... seals – they ate the meat and made clothes from the fur. Many of the people still (4) .... seal-skin clothes today because they are very warm. Remember, the weather is extremely cold for many months of the year.

Mariano Tagalik, a 65-year-old Inuit, told us a little about her early life. 'Our winter igloos were very warm. We (5) .... inside, so sometimes it got too hot. When I was a child, I (6) .... most of my clothes when I was in our igloo. In the short summers, we lived in seal-skin tents, but I (7) .... as much time as possible playing outside.'

To move over the snow, Inuit people (8) .... special snowshoes on their feet, but today many Inuits (9) .... snowmobiles. These machines can travel long distances in a short time. In the past, it (10) .... them days or weeks to travel the same distance.

Inuit children never went to school – they learnt everything from their parents, but now, like all North Americans, they (11) .... to school for about ten years. Life is not as hard as it (12) ...., but many of the older Inuits (13) .... modern life and want to go back to the old days.

3 Complete the conversation. Use the positive, negative or question form of **there is/are** or **it is**.

JANE: *(standing outside a restaurant)* This is the new Mexican restaurant.

MARY: (1) .....Is it..... expensive?

JANE: No, I don't think so. Look, (2) .... an empty table. Let's go in.

MARY: OK. *(walking into the restaurant)* Mm, (3) .... very noisy.

JANE: That's because (4) .... a man with a guitar over there – look.

MARY: Oh yes, and (5) .... some Mexican dancers too.

JANE: Great! I like dancing. (6) .... somewhere we can put our coats?

MARY: Yes, by the door ... Let's have a look at the menu. Mmm, (7) .... a lot of things that I don't understand. I mean, what's guacamole?

JANE: I don't know, but we can ask the waiter.

MARY: Excuse me, could you tell me what guacamole is, please?

WAITER: Avocado, tomatoes, ...

JANE: (8) .... any nuts in it? I can't eat nuts – I'm allergic to them.

WAITER: No, (9) .... any nuts in it.

MARY: (10) .... hot or cold?

WAITER: Cold.

MARY: OK, two guacamoles, to start with. Then what, Jane?

JANE: (11) .... a vegetarian dish on the menu, unfortunately, so ...

WAITER: Excuse me, try fajitas. (12) .... a vegetarian dish, made with beans.

MARY: Great, so two fajitas as well, then.

4 Complete this email from Nina, who lives in Britain, to Martin, her Australian friend. Use **it is(n't)/was(n't)** or **there is(n't)/was(n't)**.

From: Nina Lester
To: Martin Jones
Subject: British weather

Hi Martin

What a strange country I live in! The weather yesterday was amazing. In the north of England (1) .....there was..... snow. (2) .... unusual to have snow in the spring there. But last winter, when everybody wanted to go skiing, (3) .... any snow at all. Here in Oxford (4) .... very windy yesterday – but that's normal. (5) .... often a strong wind in spring, but yesterday (6) .... really cold too. My sister lives on the east side of the country, and she said that yesterday (7) .... really dark in the middle of the afternoon and (8) .... a storm. It frightened her kids. Today is different again! (9) .... cloudy. (10) .... no rain yet, but I know (11) .... coming. Yeah – the first drop has just landed on the window!

Nina

95 Write short questions (**Do you**, **Isn't it** etc.).

1 I said something very stupid yesterday.

....Did you.... ? What was it?

2 I don't want to talk to that man over there.

.... ? Why not?

3 My husband can't cook at all.

.... ? Is that a problem for you?

4 You forgot to phone me yesterday.

.... ? I'm sorry.

5 My wife doesn't like football.

.... ? Why not?

6 I haven't met any new people recently.

.... ? What a pity.

7 I'm not going to eat anything tonight.

.... ? Are you on a diet?

8 My son was ill last week.

.... ? Is he better now?

9 I was wrong about Adam.

.... ? In what way?

10 Jane has just agreed to marry me!

.... ? Congratulations!

96 Jon Clark is interviewing actor, Emma Pierce. Complete the conversation with positive question tags (**is it?**, **can you?** etc.) or negative question tags (**weren't you?**, **hasn't it?** etc.).

JON: Now, you were born in Alaska, (1) ....weren't you.... ?

EMMA: Yes, that's right.

JON: And then you all moved to New York, (2) .... ?

EMMA: Well, no. We moved to Los Angeles first, then to New York.

JON: OK, but you don't live in New York now, (3) .... ?

EMMA: No. My family do, but I live in Atlanta.

JON: I see. Now, you've got two brothers, (4) .... ? And you're all actors.
       That's very unusual, (5) .... ?

EMMA: I guess so, but my parents were both actors, so …

JON: They weren't very happy about you becoming an actor, (6) .... ?

EMMA: No, not at first. They wanted one of their children to do something different. But now
       they're really pleased about my success.

JON: I know you've acted with your brothers in a film, but you haven't made a film with
       your parents, (7) .... ?

EMMA: Not yet, but we're hoping to do one together next year.

JON: Fascinating. Tell me more.

7 A journalist from a music magazine asked Tim Drake and Damian Sutton, two members of the band 'Jamba', some questions. Read their answers.

		TIM	*DAMIAN*
1	Are you interested in sport?	yes	no – boring
2	Do you have a girlfriend at the moment?	no	yes – Nina
3	Were you good at school?	yes	no – left at 16
4	Did you go to university?	yes	no – worked in bank for two years
5	Do you enjoy listening to other bands?	yes	no – no time
6	Have you been to many countries?	no	yes – favourite place Jamaica

Now complete the article in the magazine.

Did you know? ...   Tim and Damian, from 'Jamba'

1 • Tim _is interested in sport, but Damian isn't._ He thinks it's boring.
2 • Tim _____ She's called Nina.
3 • Tim _____ He left when he was 16.
4 • Tim _____ He worked in a bank for two years.
5 • Tim _____ He has no time.
6 • Tim _____ His favourite place is Jamaica.

8 Mark has gone to see Madame Petra. A lot of what she says is wrong. Mark tells Madame Petra where she's wrong. Complete what he says with verbs in the negative form.

I think your name begins with an 'a', maybe Andreas or Aaron. You were born in England, but you lived in Germany when you were younger. You can speak four languages. You're married and you've got two children. Your wife is a scientist, I think. Your parents live in your house with you and your family. Your son will be 14 next birthday.

You're wrong about me. My name (1) _isn't Andreas_ . It's Mark. I (2) _____ in England. I was born in Canada. I (3) _____ in Germany when I was younger. We lived in the USA. I (4) _____ four languages. I can only speak two. Yes, I'm married, but I (5) _____ two children – only one who's called Tony. My wife (6) _____ a scientist. She's a teacher, and my parents (7) _____ with us – they live in their own house. My son (8) _____ 14 next birthday. He'll be 10.

65

99 Read this information and complete what Meg says. Use **So** (**So can I** etc.) or **Neither** (**Neither have I** etc.) or **I** (**I'm not** etc.).

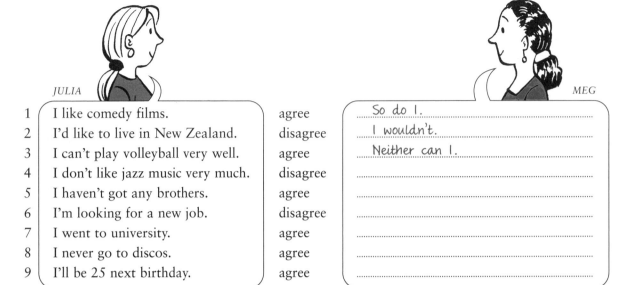

JULIA

MEG

1	I like comedy films.	agree	So do I.
2	I'd like to live in New Zealand.	disagree	I wouldn't.
3	I can't play volleyball very well.	agree	Neither can I.
4	I don't like jazz music very much.	disagree	
5	I haven't got any brothers.	agree	
6	I'm looking for a new job.	disagree	
7	I went to university.	agree	
8	I never go to discos.	agree	
9	I'll be 25 next birthday.	agree	

Sheila introduced Julia and Meg to each other. Complete Sheila's email to her brother, John. Only write about the things that Meg agrees with. Use **So … Meg** or **Neither … Meg**.

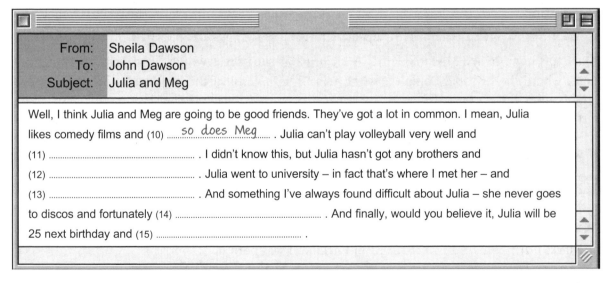

From: Sheila Dawson
To: John Dawson
Subject: Julia and Meg

Well, I think Julia and Meg are going to be good friends. They've got a lot in common. I mean, Julia likes comedy films and (10) .... *so does Meg* .... Julia can't play volleyball very well and (11) .... I didn't know this, but Julia hasn't got any brothers and (12) .... Julia went to university – in fact that's where I met her – and (13) .... And something I've always found difficult about Julia – she never goes to discos and fortunately (14) .... And finally, would you believe it, Julia will be 25 next birthday and (15) ....

And what about you? Are you the same as Meg or Julia? Write true answers about yourself. Use **so** (**so do I** etc.) and **neither** (**neither do I** etc.).

Julia and Meg like comedy films and so do I.

Meg wouldn't like to live in New Zealand and neither would I.

....

....

....

....

is it ... ?   have you ... ?   do they ... ?
(questions)

0 You are asking Jack some questions. Write the questions.

YOU

JACK

1	(live?)	Where do you live	?	In the middle of the town.
2	(do?)		?	I'm a teacher.
3	(university?)		?	Yes, I studied physics.
4	(married?)		?	Yes, I am.
5	(meet your wife?)		?	At a wedding!
6	(any children?)		?	Yes, a daughter called Emily.
7	(Emily / to school?)		?	No, not yet. She's only three.
8	(your wife work?)		?	Yes, at home. She looks after Emily.
9	(enjoy your job?)		?	Yes, most of the time.
10	(holiday?)		?	Eleven weeks a year.

1 This is the scene at Emily's party. Complete the questions.

1 There's some wonderful food over there.
   Mmm. Who ....made.... it? (make)

2 I went to the cinema last night.
   What ....did you see.... ? (see)

3 I'm going to tell Maria that I don't want to meet her again.
   What .... to her? (say)

4 ... and then just at that moment, a man opened the window and started to climb in.
   What .... next? (happen)

5 Well, Julia likes Simon, but he doesn't really like her. Someone else does.
   Really? Who .... Julia? (like)

6 I heard that Carmen is getting married next month.
   I didn't know that. Who .... you that? (tell)

7 I can hear music coming from next door.
   Me too. Who .... the piano? (play)

102 Andy Perkins is a private investigator. He is watching someone in the park and he's reporting what he can see to his colleague in his office. His colleague is writing down some questions. Complete the questions. Each question ends with a preposition (**to, for, at, with** etc.).

Andy

'The woman is here again. She's sitting on the bench and (1) she's writing a letter, I think. (2) I don't think she's from Britain. She keeps looking at her watch – maybe (3) she's waiting for someone. Oh, now (4) she's talking on her mobile. Yesterday when she was here, she had a dog with her. (5) It didn't belong to her. It belonged to someone else. I know because she looked very uncomfortable with it. But no dog today.

   Now over by the trees, there's a man. He's been standing there and (6) looking at something for a long time. Now the woman is standing up and walking in his direction. They've just shaken hands and now (7) they're talking. They're leaving the park. I must follow them.

1 Who __'s she writing to__ ?
2 Where .... ?
3 Who .... ?
4 Who .... ?
5 Who .... ?
6 What .... ?
7 What .... ?

3 Read each conversation and complete the questions.

1 RACHEL: ....*Did you*..... enjoy your holiday?

    DAVE: Yes, thanks. It was wonderful.

    RACHEL: .... go?

    DAVE: To Jamaica.

    RACHEL: .... go with?

    DAVE: Two friends from college.

    RACHEL: .... the weather like?

    DAVE: Sunny every day.

2 ROB: .... done?

    DAN: I've broken my arm.

    ROB: .... do it?

    DAN: I fell off my bike.

    ROB: .... hurt?

    DAN: Not now, but it did.

3 BRUNO: We can catch the next Manchester train if we hurry.

    ELLA: .... leave?

    BRUNO: Half past nine, from Central Station.

    ELLA: .... take?

    BRUNO: About two hours. We should be there just after 11.30. So hurry up!

    ELLA: I'm nearly ready. .... wear – the
                 brown one or the black one?

    BRUNO: I like your black jacket best.

    ELLA: OK, then I'm ready.

4 Find the mistakes in these sentences. Correct the sentences.

1 What time <u>leaves</u> the train?   *What time does the train leave?*

2 Why you didn't ring me last night?   ....

3 To who are you giving that present?   ....

4 How much has spent Mary?   ....

5 Where did Jo went for her holidays last year? ....

6 How long takes it to get to your school?   ....

7 What do you usually in the evenings?   ....

8 What did happen yesterday evening?   ....

9 When was built the Taj Mahal?   ....

69

105 Marta is phoning her friend, Silvia. Use the words to complete the conversation. Do not change the form of the words.

MARTA: Hi Silvia. (1) anything / you / doing / tonight / are?
         Are you doing anything tonight   ?

SILVIA: No, nothing special. Why?

MARTA: I'd like to go to the cinema.

SILVIA: (2) to see / do / want / you / what?
                                                                                            ?

MARTA: 'Casablanca'. It's an old film. (3) it / you / have / seen?
                                                                                            ?

SILVIA: Yes. I went last night – sorry.

MARTA: Oh, what a pity. (4) did / who / go / with / you?
                                                                                            ?

SILVIA: My mum. She's seen it five times.

MARTA: (5) like / was / what / it?
                                                                                            ?

SILVIA: Good – I cried at the end. Anyway, (6) you / to do / like / else / would / something?
                                                                                            ?

MARTA: Yeah, OK. (7) you / come / why / to my house / don't?
                                                                                            ?

         I'll cook dinner for you. My parents are away at the moment.

SILVIA: That sounds great. (8) going / are / how long / away / they / to be?
                                                                                            ?

MARTA: Just until the weekend.

SILVIA: (9) anything / I / for dinner / bring / can?
                                                                                            ?

MARTA: No, nothing – just yourself. Come early, because I need to tell you something.

SILVIA: Really? (10) you / to me / do / to talk / want / what / about?
                                                                                            ?

MARTA: I'll tell you when I see you.

SILVIA: OK. See you later. Oh by the way, (11) to your house / to walk / it / how long / from the station / does / take?
                                                                                            ?

         Last time I came, I was driving.

MARTA: It's only about ten minutes.

SILVIA: OK. See you soon. Bye.

6 Carla has emailed her friend Charlotte some questions about another friend, Juan. Unfortunately, Charlotte doesn't know the answers to Carla's questions!

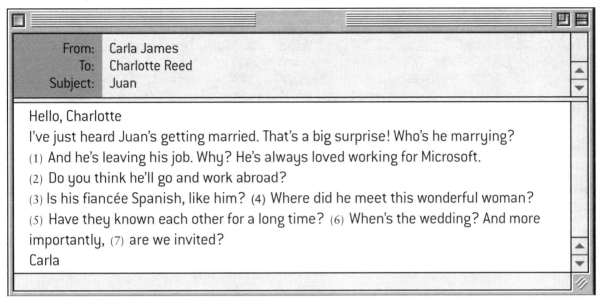

From: Carla James
To: Charlotte Reed
Subject: Juan

Hello, Charlotte
I've just heard Juan's getting married. That's a big surprise! Who's he marrying?
(1) And he's leaving his job. Why? He's always loved working for Microsoft.
(2) Do you think he'll go and work abroad?
(3) Is his fiancée Spanish, like him? (4) Where did he meet this wonderful woman?
(5) Have they known each other for a long time? (6) When's the wedding? And more importantly, (7) are we invited?
Carla

Complete Charlotte's answers. Use **I don't know**.

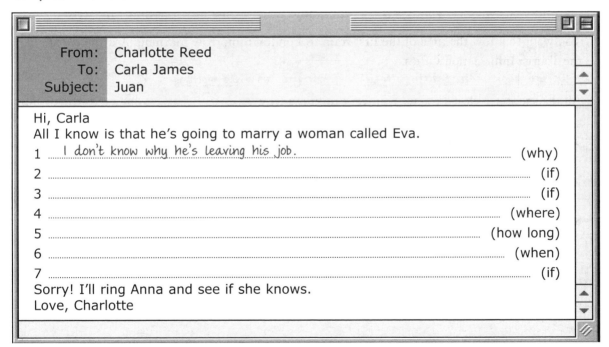

From: Charlotte Reed
To: Carla James
Subject: Juan

Hi, Carla
All I know is that he's going to marry a woman called Eva.
1   _I don't know why he's leaving his job._ (why)
2   .... (if)
3   .... (if)
4   .... (where)
5   .... (how long)
6   .... (when)
7   .... (if)
Sorry! I'll ring Anna and see if she knows.
Love, Charlotte

107   Some words in this report are difficult to read. Ask questions to find the missing information. Use **Do you know … ?**

> John Carter left home at (1) /////// yesterday morning. He was wearing a
> (2) /////// and a /////// . He wasn't alone. (3) /////// was with him. First
> he went into a shop and bought a camera. It cost (4) /////// . Then he
> went into a (5) /////// shop and came out carrying a long, thin package.
> The person with him was laughing, probably because (6) /////// . They
> walked to the station and caught the fast train which was going to
> (7) /////// .

1   Do you know what time John Carter left home yesterday morning?

2   ....

3   ....

4   ....

5   ....

6   ....

7   ....

108   Write questions with **Do you know** (**Do you know when / how much / what / if** etc.).

1   You want to know the time of the first train to London tomorrow morning. Ask the person in the Tourist Information Office.

     Do you know when the first train to London is tomorrow morning ?

2   All the shops are closed today. You want to know why. Ask.

     .... ?

3   You want to find the Regent Hotel. You ask a stranger in the street.

     .... ?

4   You want to go to a concert, but you don't know the cost of the tickets. Ask a friend.

     .... ?

5   Someone told you that Mr Collins, your old teacher, has died. You want to know when.

     .... ?

6   You want to go to a Chinese restaurant, but you don't want to walk very far. Ask a stranger if there is one nearby.

     .... ?

109   You're on holiday in New York. Write four questions you might ask at the Tourist Information Office. Use **Do you know** (**Do you know when / how much / what / if** etc.).

     .... ?

     .... ?

     .... ?

     .... ?

She said that ...   He told me that ...
(reported speech)

0 Tim invited some people to his and Maria's party on Saturday.

CAROLINE

I'm working really hard. I don't have time to go out in the evening.

STEPHEN

I've got a few days' holiday. I'm going to Italy.

DAVE

I'm ill. I've been in bed for two days.

ANNA

I don't like parties. I can't dance.

TONY

My sister's arriving from Australia on Saturday and I'm going to meet her at the airport.

SUE

I love parties. I'll be free on Saturday.

Now complete what Tim said later to Maria.

MARIA: Did you invite Caroline to our party on Saturday?

TIM: Yes, but she can't come. She said
(1) *she was working really hard* and
(2) *she didn't have time to go out in the evening* .

MARIA: OK. What about Stephen?

TIM: No. He said (3) ....
and (4) ....

MARIA: Dave?

TIM: No. He said (5) ....
and (6) ....

MARIA: Anna?

TIM: No, not Anna. She said (7) ....
and (8) ....

MARIA: Can Tony come?

TIM: No. He said (9) ....
and (10) ....

MARIA: What about Sue?

TIM: Yes. She said (11) ....
and (12) ....

MARIA: Great! That's a start!

111   At the office, Jane's manager is looking for her. Read what these people say.

	MANAGER:	Where's Jane?
1	CLARE:	She's in the photocopy room.
	MANAGER:	No, she's not. I've looked there.
2	PAUL:	She doesn't work here on Mondays.
	MANAGER:	Really, that's news to me.
3	STUART:	She's gone out.
	MANAGER:	Where to?
4	SIMON:	She's at lunch. She'll be back soon.
	MANAGER:	At half past three in the afternoon?
5	MIKE:	She leaves early on Mondays.
	MANAGER:	Nobody leaves early on Mondays.
6	DIANA:	She's making a cup of tea.
	MANAGER:	Come on, Mary. You tell me. Where's Jane?
7	MARY:	I don't know where she is.

Half an hour later, Jane's manager finds her. Complete the conversation.

MANAGER: Oh Jane. You're here. I asked everyone where you were.

(1) ...Clare said you were in the photocopy room...

(2) ....

(3) ....

(4) .... and ....

(5) ....

(6) ....

(7) ....

So, where were you?

(Finish with your own ideas.)

JANE: (8) I was ....

2 Which alternative is correct?

1 Could I ......**B**...... your dictionary, please?
   A borrowing   B borrow   C to borrow

2 Why is that car .... outside our house?
   A stopping   B stop   C to stop

3 You don't look well. You should .... to bed.
   A going   B go   C to go

4 Do we have .... now? I'm enjoying myself.
   A leaving   B leave   C to leave

5 'Shall I .... off the TV?' 'Yes, please.'
   A turning   B turn   C to turn

6 I must .... my postcards today. We're leaving on Friday.
   A writing   B write   C to write

7 You didn't need .... any more eggs. We had some in the fridge.
   A buying   B buy   C to buy

8 We used .... a dog, but it died last year.
   A having   B have   C to have

9 My brother wants .... a teacher when he finishes college.
   A being   B be   C to be

10 'What would you like .... tonight?' 'Let's go out for a walk.'
   A doing   B do   C to do

3 Complete the letter with the to ... or –ing form of the verbs.

Dear Francesca

Thank you for your last letter. It was good to hear from you. My big news is that I've decided
(1) ......**to change**...... (change) jobs. I finish (2) ......**working**...... (work) at Simpsons next month and
start in my new company, Galt, the week after. Simpsons didn't want me (3) ....
(go), but Galt offered me more money and more opportunities. I hope (4) .... (be) a
manager there in two years.

   By the way, I forgot (5) .... (tell) you – I'm learning (6) ....
(drive). My new company offered (7) .... (let) me use one of their cars, which was
very good of them. I had a lot of problems at first because I wanted (8) .... (do)
everything quickly. My teacher thought I was a bit dangerous on the road! He suggested
(9) .... (slow) down, and now it's getting better.

   I'm having a party on the 25th and would love (10) .... (see) you. Perhaps you
could persuade your sister (11) .... (come) with you as well. I really enjoyed
(12) .... (talk) to her at your party. My neighbours have promised
(13) .... (go) out for the evening, so we can play the music as loud as we want.
   I must stop (14) .... (write) now and do some work. See you on the
25th, I hope.

Love, Carolina

114   Complete the second sentence in each pair. Use **to** if necessary.

1 The doctor said I should stop eating chocolate.
The doctor *advised me to stop eating chocolate.* (advise)

2 I said to David, 'Don't play with that knife.'
I .... (tell)

3 Stuart didn't allow his young sons to play with toy guns.
Stuart .... (let)

4 Jane didn't want to come swimming with us, but we asked her again and she said 'yes'.
We .... (persuade)

5 I was surprised that you failed the exam.
I .... (expect)

6 My father said I had to pay back all the money I borrowed.
My father .... (make)

115   Complete the questions with **do / to do / doing**.

1 What do you hope *to do* when you finish studying?
2 When you were younger, what did your parents make you .... ?
3 What did your parents never let you .... ?
4 Is there a job in the house that you don't mind .... ?
5 What have you always wanted .... , but never had the time or money?
6 What do you most enjoy .... when you want to relax?
7 If you could have any job, what would you like .... ?

Now answer the questions for yourself.

1 *I hope to have a long holiday when I finish studying.*
2 ....
3 ....
4 ....
5 ....
6 ....
7 ....

116   Finish the sentences with **to (do something)** or **for (something)**. Use your own ideas.

1 Tanya went upstairs to *wash her hair.*
2 Jack went upstairs for *a book.*
3 I wrote to Maria to ....
4 Manuel is going to call the airport for ....
5 I need some more money ....
6 Kate's going to the kitchen ....
7 Lucy didn't have enough time ....
8 Gina waited a long time ....

7 Two alternatives are correct. Cross out the wrong alternative.

1 I   would like   to meet Lisa.
           don't want
           ~~suggest~~

2 My sister   doesn't mind   swimming in the sea.
               wants me
               likes

3 Stella's boss   made   her work late.
                   asked
                   let

4 Did you   use   to play the piano when you were younger?
             learn
             finish

5 Matthias   started   learning Spanish as well as English.
              decided
              suggested

6 I   forgot   to buy some bread.
           don't need
           don't mind

7 David   told   me not to speak so loudly.
           made
           advised

8 Complete the sentences with the correct form of the verbs.

JANE: What are you doing this weekend?

PAT: Well, on Saturday we're going (1) ....*swimming*...... (swim). Do you want
       (2) .....*to come*..... (come) with us?

JANE: I can't swim if someone isn't (3) .... (hold) me. I've been thinking of
       (4) .... (have) lessons.

PAT: Well, I can help you. I taught Karen (5) .... (swim).

JANE: Did you? OK, I'll come. Would you like me (6) .... (bring) a picnic?

SARA: What did you do after (7) .... (leave) school?

ROB: I studied law. My father is a lawyer and he persuaded me (8) .... (go) to
       law school.

SARA: Did you enjoy it?

ROB: Not really, because it wasn't my choice. My father made me (9) .... (do) it.
       I wanted (10) .... (go) to college (11) .... (study) journalism.
       So after two years of law school I left without (12) .... (tell) my father and
       went to live in France.

SARA: And now you work for a French newspaper in London.

ROB: That's right, and I love it.

119 Complete the story with the correct form of **do** or **make**.

Today was my first day back at work after my holiday. Halfway through the morning I thought, 'I've got so much (1) __to do__ that I've forgotten my holiday already.' The company I work for (2) __makes__ chairs – not really the most exciting things in the world. My job is well-paid, but I don't think I'll (3) .... it for much longer.

I went into the office kitchen and (4) .... myself a cup of coffee. Then, I went back to my office and (5) .... a few phone calls. At lunchtime, I went to the park. I always (6) .... some sandwiches before I come to work in the mornings. I prefer not to eat too much at lunchtime because John always (7) .... something delicious for dinner.

The afternoon passed quickly. I (8) .... a list of all the things I had to (9) .... the next day. Then at 6 o'clock, the phone rang. It was my boss. 'Sally, what are you (10) .... tomorrow? Do you think you could (11) .... me a favour?'

'Sure,' I answered. 'What is it you want me (12) .... ?'

'Could you take Dave Turner out for lunch? He's the buyer from Martins. I've (13) .... an appointment to see my accountant at 1 o'clock and I don't want to cancel it.'

'OK, I'll (14) .... it.' But I knew I was (15) .... a big mistake. I didn't like Dave Turner and I don't think he liked me either.

At home that evening, I helped my son (16) .... his homework. Then we all had dinner together. Afterwards, John (17) .... the washing-up and I (18) .... the ironing.

I slept badly that night, but in the morning I knew what I had (19) .... I wasn't happy in my job. It was time for a big talk with my boss.

120 What do you say in these situations? Use the correct form of **have** (or **have got**).

1 Your friend, Lorenzo, has just come back from his holiday. Ask him about it.
   (a good holiday) __Did you have a good holiday__ ?

2 Your brother looks very red and hot. What do you ask him?
   (a temperature) .... ?

3 Your mother is preparing lunch for everyone today. Ask her what you're going to eat.
   (lunch today) .... ?

4 There's a problem with your computer. Ask your brother to check it.
   (a look) .... ?

5 David has just got a new job. You know he changes work quite often. Ask him about his jobs.
   (How many) .... ?

6 You and a friend need some exercise. Suggest a walk later.
   (Shall) .... ?

I me my mine myself
(pronouns and possessives)

1 Complete the sentences. Use **I/she/they** etc. and **them/him/you** etc.

'Hi. I'm Josie Clark. This is Pete. (1) ......He...... 's my best friend and I like
(2) .... very much. Pete and (3) .... aren't British.
(4) .... 're from San Francisco. (5) .... 's a beautiful
city on the west coast of North America. Last autumn, Pete came on
holiday with (6) .... to Yellowstone National Park. In this
photo, (7) .... 's watching some bears. We were lucky to see
(8) .... because at that time of year (9) .... were
getting ready to go to sleep for the winter.'

Complete the sentences. Use **I/me/my/mine**, **you/your/yours** and
he/him/his etc.

'And in this photo you can see the bridge. San Francisco is famous for
(10) .... bridge – the Golden Gate Bridge. I'm lucky because
(11) .... family live near the bridge. From (12) ....
sitting room window we can see it. It's great – especially at night.
(13) .... brother, Sam, lives with (14) .... wife, Laura,
and (15) .... two kids about two kilometres from us. Laura is
from Uruguay, and (16) .... parents still live there.'

2 Complete the letter. Use **I/me/my/mine**, **you/your/yours** and **he/him/his** etc.

Dear Ellie

Thank you for (1) .....your..... card. It was good to hear from (2) .... and to know

(3) .... news. Let (4) .... tell you my news. In June, (5) .... sister,

Isabel, is getting married to Joe. Do you remember? I met Joe ten years ago, so he's an old

friend of (6) .... (7) .... 're getting married in the afternoon and my parents

are having a big party for (8) .... in the evening. Isabel's not been well recently, so

(9) .... 'm really happy for (10) .... , and for Joe too. After the wedding,

they're coming to stay with (11) .... because they haven't got an apartment yet. So we'll

be one big, happy family.

　　My good friend, Pete, is taking (12) .... final exams next month. After that,

(13) .... wants to get a job in a hospital. I think it'll be difficult for (14) .... ,

but he really wants to be a doctor. Good luck to (15) .... !

　　Last week I met Jane and Tina Sarton. Do you remember (16) .... ?

(17) .... brother was at school with us. I gave Jane your telephone number and she gave

me (18) .... Perhaps we can all meet sometime soon.

　　I must stop now. By the way, I found a silver pen in my room. It's not (19) ....

Is it (20) .... ? I know you've got a silver one. My parents send (21) ....

love to you and (22) .... parents.

Love, Liz

123 Complete the sentences. Use **himself/themselves** etc., **by myself / by herself** etc. or **each other**.

1 Jack was very surprised when he looked at ......*himself*...... in the mirror.
2 I don't like going to the cinema with other people. I prefer going .....*by myself*..... .
3 Joe loves Tina and Tina loves Joe. They love ....*each other*.... .
4 The child had no brothers or sisters, so she often had to play ....
5 My husband and I went to the same school when we were children, so we saw
   .... very often.
6 'Are you talking to me?' 'No, I'm talking to .... !'
7 Paul and Mike have known .... for ten years.

124 Complete the sentences. Use **himself/themselves** etc., **by myself / by herself** etc. or **each other** and the verbs from the box.

| cut   enjoyed   ~~lived~~   understand   went   wrote |

1 Carlo .....*lived by himself*..... in a large house by the sea.
2 I'm afraid that the children are going to
   .... on the broken glass.
3 Marie speaks only French and Jill speaks
   only English, so they can't ....
4 Eva didn't go to Madrid with anyone.
   She ....
5 We had a great time in London together. We really ....
6 Marianne and Catherine were penfriends for a long time. They .... to
   .... every week for five years.

125 There are mistakes in ten of these sentences. Correct the sentences where necessary. Write 'OK' if the sentence is already correct.

1 Is this book <u>your</u>?   *Is this book yours?*
2 Meg and I have known <u>us</u> for five years.   *Meg and I have known each other*
                                                                for five years.

3 James gave me those books. I really like it.   ....
4 Some friends of them told them the news.   ....
5 Pat gave her brother a DVD and he gave she a book.   ....
6 My sister and her husband don't love themselves   ....
   any more. They aren't happy together.   ....
7 John is a good friend of me.   ....
8 It's your decision, not ours.   ....
9 I like this house, but her windows are broken.   ....
10 I know Mary, but I don't know his brother.   ....
11 I sometimes ask me why I work in a noisy city.   ....

6 Complete the second sentence. Use -'s or -s' + a noun.

1 Adam and Claudia are husband and wife. Adam is ....Claudia's husband.... .

2 This car belongs to Anne. It's ....

3 I was with Elena at her house last night. I was at .... last night.

4 All the students have put their books on the table. All .... are on the table.

5 My sister was born on the 28th of June. The 28th of June is ....

6 Mrs Penn makes delicious cakes. .... are delicious.

7 My grandparents have a house next door to us. My .... is next door to ours.

8 Jenny and Mark Smith have a daughter, Chris. Jenny and Mark are ....

7 This is Mike and Alan's room. Whose are the objects in the room? Are they Mike's or Alan's?

Mike likes: football, motorbikes, chocolate, wild animals
Alan likes: reading, playing the guitar, computer games, running

1 ....The elephant poster is Mike's......... 5 ....

2 .... 6 ....

3 .... 7 ....

4 .... 8 ....

8 Complete the sentences. Use -'s/-s' or the ... of ... .

1 What's ....the name of this street............ ? (the name / this street)

2 When's ....Alice's birthday............ ? (the birthday / Alice)

3 Which is .... ? (the favourite team / John)

4 What's .... ? (the result / the match)

5 When's .... ? (the anniversary party / your parents)

6 How big are .... ? (the windows / the house)

7 What's .... ? (the telephone number / the station)

8 Do you know .... ? (the daughter / Mark Turner)

a/an and some
(singular and plural)

129 Write the opposites. Use **a** or **an**.

1 a big house
  a small house

2 a full glass

3 an easy question

4 a new book

5 a cold day

6 an expensive hotel

7 an old man

8 a light bag

9 a boring film

130 Write answers to the quiz questions. Use plural nouns.

1 People use these to cut meat with.   _knives_
2 People wear these to tell the time.   w
3 We eat these round red fruits in salads.   t
4 You stand and walk on these important parts of the body.   f
5 You brush these after you've eaten.   t
6 Half the world are men. What are the other half?   w............
7 These people are between the ages of 3 and 12.   c
8 When these little people are born, their parents are happy.   b
9 We get wool from these animals.   s
10 There are seven of these in a week.   d

131 Which alternatives are correct? Sometimes only one alternative is correct, and sometimes two alternatives are possible. Cross out the wrong alternatives.

1 Mary's got .... which comes half way down her back.
  A long hair   B ~~long hairs~~   C ~~a long hair~~
2 There's .... about English courses at the back of the book. It's very useful.
  A some information   B an information   C some informations
3 It's .... today, isn't it? Let's go for a swim.
  A beautiful weather   B a beautiful weather   C a beautiful day
4 My son gave me .... for my birthday. It smells lovely.
  A a perfume   B some perfume   C a bottle of perfume
5 I don't usually buy .... in the morning, but I did this morning. There was an interesting story in it.
  A a paper   B paper   C some paper
6 'Why is Jane crying?' 'She's just had ....'
  A some bad news   B a bad news   C a bad new
7 Jake is really happy. He's got .... in a multi-national company. It's a big change from his old one.
  A new job   B a new work   C a new job
8 I've got .... to do tonight, so I can't come to the cinema with you.
  A work   B some work   C a work

2 The Campbell family are packing their suitcases for their summer holiday. Complete the lists.
Use a(n), some or a pair of / two pairs of ... .

1 John is taking
   two pairs of shorts
   a hat
   some towels
   ....

2 Sarah is taking
   ....
   ....
   ....
   ....

3 Mrs Campbell is taking
   ....
   ....
   ....
   ....

4 Mr Campbell is taking
   ....
   ....
   ....
   ....

And what about you? Next month you're going on holiday for three weeks to Australia (or the
mountains of South America, or Florida). Write six things that you're going to take with you.

I'm going to take ....

....

133 Write **a/an** or **the**.

1 William wrote ......*a*..... letter to his bank yesterday, but he forgot to post it. This morning, he
   saw ....*the*...... letter on the kitchen table.

2 When Eva White was younger, she wanted to be .... musician. Now many people
   think she's .... best trumpet player in the world.

3 I've got .... idea. Let's go to .... new Greek restaurant in Main Street tonight.

4 Julia arrived at .... station at 7 o'clock and took .... taxi to ....
   city centre.

5 We usually eat our meals in .... kitchen. But if we have .... guest, we eat in
   .... dining room.

6 Bangkok is .... capital of Thailand. It's .... large city with about 8 million
   inhabitants.

7 I work in Montreal. My office is on .... third floor of .... old building.

8 Martin lives in .... large town in .... middle of Germany, but he wants to
   live in .... country. He's got .... dog and he'd like to take .... dog
   for long walks.

9 I've known my husband, Sam, since I was six. We lived in .... same street when we
   were children. Sam had .... older brother, Frank. I thought he was .... most
   handsome boy in the world.

10 A: Excuse me, where's .... nearest bookshop?
    B: It's at .... end of this street, on .... left. There's .... bus
        stop in front of it.

134 Read the story. There is a word missing in some lines. Write **a(n)** or **the** where necessary.
Write 'OK' if the line is already complete.

Last night, moon was shining brightly. Clare's train	(1) ....*the moon*....
arrived at the station and she got off. She went up	(2) ...*OK*....
to station manager and asked, 'Do you know if there	(3) ....
is Italian restaurant near here?' 'Yes, it's very	(4) ....
near, just about 200 metres on left, opposite	(5) ....
Information Centre.' 'Thank you,' said Clare and	(6) ....
she started walking. She found restaurant and went	(7) ....
inside. There was woman playing the piano, and	(8) ....
there, in the corner of the room next to kitchen, was	(9) ....
Ron Allen – man she wanted to see. He was eating	(10) ....
dinner, but he stopped when he saw Clare. He thought	(11) ....
she looked exactly same – beautiful and calm. 'Have	(12) ....
you got papers?' he asked. 'No, I haven't. I've given	(13) ....
them to police,' she replied. 'I hope they will arrest	(14) ....
you and send you to prison.' When he heard her words,	(15) ....
Ron jumped up, took a knife from table and ran out.	(16) ....

5 A journalist is interviewing Michael Winterton, who is a travel writer. Write **the** where necessary. If **the** is not necessary, leave an empty space (–).

INTERVIEWER: When did your interest in (1) ....–........ travel start?

MICHAEL: Well, I wasn't interested in it at all until I was 15. Then I read a book about (2) ......the...... history of the South American Indians, and that got me started.

INTERVIEWER: Do you spend a lot of time travelling?

MICHAEL: Yes, I'm probably away from (3) .... home about 50 per cent of (4) .... year. And I get really fed up with staying in (5) .... hotels. But .... (6) hotel I stayed in last month in Sweden was a bit different – it was made of (7) .... ice. I must show you (8) .... photos my wife took of it. She's good at taking (9) .... photos.

INTERVIEWER: Tell me about your likes and dislikes.

MICHAEL: Well, I enjoy listening to (10) .... music, but to be honest I don't really like (11) .... music my son plays on his guitar. Watching (12) .... football is another of my hobbies. I support (13) .... my local club. And I love (14) .... food. When I visit foreign countries, I always go to local restaurants and try dishes which are typical of that region. The only thing I don't eat is (15) .... cheese – I hate it!

6 Here is some information about London. Put in **the** where necessary before the names of the famous places. If **the** is not necessary, leave an empty space (–).

Most tourists want to see where the Queen lives when they visit (1) ....–........ London, so (2) .... Buckingham Palace is very popular. But I think the best thing to do is to take a boat trip on (3) .... River Thames to see all the famous buildings. You can get on the boat at (4) .... Westminster Bridge, near (5) .... Houses of Parliament. If you go down the river to (6) .... Tower of London, you'll pass (7) .... St Paul's Cathedral on the way. This is a very old and beautiful church, and my favourite building.

As a change from sightseeing, you could go shopping along (8) .... Oxford Street, or maybe if you like animals, go to (9) .... London Zoo. There's lots to do and see in the capital. Come and see!

What can tourists do and see in your capital city? Is your capital city on a river or on the coast? Write about an important street and some famous buildings that you like.

My capital city is .... I think a good thing for tourists to do is to ....

....

137 Write **some** or **any**.

DAN: Let's go for a picnic by the river tomorrow.

JUDY: OK. We'll make (1) ......*some*...... sandwiches. What do we need?

DAN: We haven't got (2) .... bread. Can you buy (3) .... ?

JUDY: Yes, sure. What about butter?

DAN: We've got (4) .... I'll buy (5) .... cheese, shall I?

JUDY: OK, and is there (6) .... orange juice in the fridge?

DAN: No, I'll get (7) ....

JUDY: Good. Do we have (8) .... apples or cherries?

DAN: We've just got apples.

JUDY: I'll get (9) .... cherries. Oh dear! I haven't got (10) .... money to buy all these things!

138 Write **someone (or somebody) / something** or **anyone (or anybody) / anything**.

1 Did ......*anyone*...... telephone me last night?

2 I feel a bit sick. I think I've eaten .... bad.

3 'What's the matter?'   'I think there's .... in the garden.'

4 'What's wrong?'   'I've put .... in my coffee and it isn't sugar!'

5 Please don't tell .... about the letter. It's a secret.

6 You look bored. Would you like .... to do?

7 There isn't .... to watch on TV tonight. Let's go out.

8 .... dropped a €50 note in the street outside my house yesterday.

9 I don't think I learnt .... from the lecture I went to.

139 Complete this conversation between John Grant and his wife, Kate. Use either **no** or **any**.

1 JOHN: I want to lie in the bath and relax for hours.

   KATE: I'm sorry, but there ...*'s no hot water*... or ...*isn't any hot water*........ . (hot water)

2 JOHN: I've been thinking, Kate. I'd really like to buy a new car this year.

   KATE: So would I, but unfortunately we .... (money)

3 JOHN: Can I have a chocolate?

   KATE: Sorry, I .... (chocolates)

4 JOHN: What about a biscuit?

   KATE: I'm afraid there .... either. (biscuits)

5 JOHN: This coffee's good, but you know I don't like it black!

   KATE: Sorry, but there .... (milk)

6 JOHN: What's for dinner tonight?

   KATE: I'm afraid we .... (food)
          Shall we go out to that new Spanish restaurant in Broad Street?

   JOHN: OK, but just let me go and change my clothes first.

   KATE: Sorry, there .... for that. (time)
          I booked a table for 9 o'clock and it's quarter to now.

There are mistakes in seven of these sentences. Correct the underlined words that are wrong.
Use **some/any/no/none**. Write 'OK' if the sentence is already correct.

1 Mary hasn't got <u>some</u> stamps in her purse.   ....any..........

2 There aren't <u>no</u> easy questions.   ....

3 'How many books did you read on holiday?' '<u>Any</u>.'   ....

4 Would you like <u>some</u> ice-cream?   ....

5 Please don't offer me chocolates. I don't want <u>none</u>.   ....

6 I didn't give him <u>no</u> help.   ....

7 Have you written <u>any</u> postcards yet?   ....

8 There are <u>any</u> biscuits in the tin. We must buy some.   ....

9 Can I have <u>any</u> potatoes, please?   ....

Complete the conversation between Jess and her friend, Sam. Use **some/any/no/none**.

JESS: Hi, Sam. How are you?

SAM: Fine, but busy. We've got (1) ......some...... exams
        next week – remember?

JESS: I know. How much work did you do last night?

SAM: (2) .... , I went to the cinema. What
        about you?

JESS: I had (3) .... time last night. It was my
        sister's birthday, so we all went out for dinner.

SAM: Have you done (4) .... this morning?

JESS: (5) .... , but not a lot. Anyway, I called to
        ask you something. Do you know where my physics
        book is?

SAM: I've got (6) .... idea, but you can borrow mine
        if you want.

JESS: Thanks.

SAM: Let's meet outside Natbank in the High Street this
        lunchtime. I need to get (7) .... money and I'll
        bring my physics book for you.

JESS: Good idea. I'm very worried about the physics exam.
        Have you got (8) .... old exam papers? I'd
        really like to look at them.

SAM: I haven't got (9) .... , but my brother's got
        (10) .... from a few years ago. I'll bring
        them with me.

JESS: Wonderful! See you at 12.30. OK?

142 Write **someone** (or **somebody**) / **anything** / **nowhere** etc.

From: Lucy Graham
To: Olivia White
Subject: Things are getting better

Hi, Olivia

I've been in this town for two months now. I haven't met (1) .....*anybody*..... interesting. Also, it's
very quiet in the evenings. All the shops and restaurants close early, and the streets are empty.
There's (2) .... to go and there's (3) .... good on the TV. That's
what I thought. Then yesterday (4) .... told me about a sports club
(5) .... near my apartment. So I decided to try it – and it's great! There's weight-
training, tennis, a swimming pool, and the people are friendly. (6) .... tells you
what to do – you can choose for yourself. In the middle of the evening, (7) ....
said, 'Hello, I'm Gina. Are you doing (8) .... later this evening? Would you like to
go for (9) .... to eat?' So we did.
Great, isn't it? I'm beginning to feel better about the town now. But it's funny, I haven't been
(10) .... for two months and then yesterday it all started to happen.
Lucy

143 Complete the sentences. Use **somebody** / **anything** / **nowhere** etc. + **to** (**to go** / **to stay** etc.).

MICHAEL: Let's have lunch in this restaurant.
MARY: It looks very busy. Is there (1) ......*anywhere to sit*...... ?
MICHAEL: Yes, there are two seats over there.

SUE: I'm hungry.
DAD: Would you like (2) .... ?
SUE: Yes, please.

LEO: I'm bored. I've got (3) ....
MUM: Go and play tennis.
LEO: All my friends are on holiday, so I haven't got (4) .... with.

LIZ: We're going to Rome in September.
JOSHUA: Wonderful.
LIZ: Yes, but we've got a problem. We haven't got (5) .... yet.
JOSHUA: Try the Plaza Hotel – they often have rooms free.

PAT: I'm going to a party at the weekend and I need (6) ....
JENNY: You can borrow my new black dress if you like.

TANYA: Gerry, go and talk to Annie. She's in the kitchen.
GERRY: I haven't got (7) ....
TANYA: Of course you have! You always have lots to say. Go and talk about food or sport.

Complete the description of Naomi's weekend with **every** or **all**.

Naomi had a bad weekend. On Friday evening, (1) ......*every*...... time she tried to sit down to eat dinner, the telephone rang. Later, she shouted at her brother John and he sat on the sofa (2) .... evening and didn't speak to anyone.

On Saturday, it rained (3) .... day, so she didn't go out. She watched a programme on TV – some kind of singing competition – but she thought that the singers were terrible. In the evening, it was still raining. But she needed some fresh air, so she went to the park. (4) .... person she saw looked wet and miserable!

That night in bed, she could hear the people in the next-door apartment. They were having a party and making a lot of noise, so she was awake (5) .... night.

On Sunday, she went to her grandmother's. She did this (6) .... Sunday, and usually she loved it. But this Sunday (7) .... the buses were late, and she arrived in a bad mood. 'I'll be happy to go back to work tomorrow,' she thought.

Write **everyone (or everybody) / everywhere / everything**.

SARAH: These shirts are expensive.
SUE: (1) ......*Everything*...... is expensive in this shop.
SARAH: And why are there so many black things? It's a very boring colour.
SUE: It's fashionable. (2) .... is wearing black this year.

DAN: Granddad says that family life was better when he was young.
MUM: Yes, a lot of old people think that (3) .... was better in the past.
DAN: And he says things in our country are changing too quickly at the moment.
MUM: Well, it's not only our country. Life is changing (4) ....

ERICA: Did you enjoy your day in London?
TIM: Yes, very much, but it was really busy (5) .... It was school holiday time and (6) .... was doing the same as us.

146   Write **of** where necessary. If **of** is not necessary, leave an empty space (–).

It was David Fallon's birthday. He was 80 years old. He sat up
in his bed and started thinking about his life.
'Most (1) ....–..... people change houses during their lifetime, but
I've lived in this house all (2) .... my life. I've got four
children and (3) all .... them were born in this house
too. Most (4) .... the time it's been a happy place to
be. The street is very different from when I was young. Then,
there were no (5) .... cars and all (6) .... the
children used to play in the road. Some (7) .... children
still do, but it's not the same – you've got to be very careful
nowadays with the traffic. None (8) .... the people
who live in the street now are as old as I am – most (9) .... them have died or moved to
another area. So I haven't any (10) .... friends here really. I don't go out much now and
I'm getting a bit deaf. But none (11) .... this is important. I've got my children and my
grandchildren, and they're everything to me.'

147   Write sentences. Use **all, most, some** or **none**.

Richard is 40 years old. He's a manager in a large multi-national company. He and the people who
work in this company answered some questions about their health.

	Yes		**Yes**
Do you take regular exercise?	78%	Have you got a car?	100%
Do you walk to work?	25%	Do you use your car every day?	80%

1   Most of Richard's colleagues take regular exercise. ....
2   ....
3   ....
4   ....

Lisa is 16 years old and she's a high school student. Read the answers that she and her friends gave
to some different questions.

	Yes		**Yes**
Do you go to the cinema every month?	20%	Do you study every night?	0%
Do you play some kind of sport?	100%	Do you enjoy dancing?	73%

5   ....
6   ....
7   ....
8   ....

What about you and your friends? Write four sentences. Use **all, most, some** or **none**.

....
....
....
....

3 This is part of a radio interview with Jamie Carpenter, writer of science fiction novels. Write **both/either/neither**. Use **of** where necessary.

INTERVIEWER: You've written many great books, but your last two weren't very successful. How did you feel about that?

JAMIE: Well, to be honest, I didn't really like (1) ...... *either of* ...... them. I wrote them in a hurry and I think it shows. (2) .... book has sold well – only 1,000 copies, which isn't good. But my latest book will be in the shops next month and I'm very pleased with it. I think it's my best one so far.

INTERVIEWER: Do you work in your house or in an office?

JAMIE: I don't work in (3) .... I have a studio at the bottom of our garden.

INTERVIEWER: Do you have any children, and do they live at home?

JAMIE: I have two girls and one boy. (4) .... girls are married, so they live with their husbands. My boy, Sam, is still living with us.

INTERVIEWER: I know you get a lot of your ideas from travelling, so can I ask you where you would like to go for a summer holiday – Thailand or Sri Lanka?

JAMIE: (5) .... them sound wonderful, don't they? But I'd choose Sri Lanka. It's somewhere I've always wanted to visit.

INTERVIEWER: When you're working, I believe that you listen to music. Do you like pop music or classical music?

JAMIE: I don't like (6) .... them. I prefer jazz.

INTERVIEWER: And what about sport? Is that an important part of your life?

JAMIE: Oh, yes. I play regularly with a team of people who are now good friends.

INTERVIEWER: Is that football or rugby?

JAMIE: (7) .... Baseball is the only sport for me. I learnt how to play it when I was living in the USA.

INTERVIEWER: Jamie Carpenter, thank you for talking to us today.

4 Write sentences about yourself and one of your friends. Think of things which are similar in your lives. Use **Both of us ... / Neither of us ... .**

Both of us live in apartments.
Neither of us has got a dog.

....
....
....
....
....
....
....

150 Look at the picture. What is left after the wedding party has finished? Write sentences. Use **There aren't many ... / There isn't much ... / There isn't/aren't any ...** .

1 There aren't many people.

2 ....

3 ....

4 ....

5 ....

6 ....

7 ....

151 Liz is asking you some questions. Write questions with **How much / many ... ?** Then write your own answers. Use **a lot, not (very) much / not (very) many, a few / a little** or **none**.

LIZ

YOU

1 books / be / on your table?
   How many books are there on your table ?   Not many.

2 milk / you like / in your coffee?
   ....?   ....

3 cars / you see / out of the window?
   ....?   ....

4 money / you spend / in one month?
   ....?   ....

5 good friends / you have?
   ....?   ....

6 water / you drink / every day?
   ....?   ....

7 pairs of socks / you have?
   ....?   ....

2 Complete the text about Antarctica. Write **little** / **a little** or **few** / **a few**.

The coldest continent

Antarctica is a snow-covered continent. The average temperature at the South Pole is –51° Celsius.
(1) ......*Few*...... plants or animals can live on the land – it is too cold for them. The animal life is found on and in the sea. There are
(2) .... scientists from different countries who live and work on special bases in Antarctica. On midsummer's day (22 December) there is daylight for 24 hours and during this period
(3) .... tourist ships and planes come to see this strange land. But in the winter there is
(4) .... daylight for months. It must be a terrible place in the winter. The snow is always there – winter and summer – but in fact (5) ....
snow falls in the year (an average of 15–20 centimetres). People say that Antarctica can be a beautiful place. At first, it appears rather frightening, but after
(6) .... time, some people fall in love with it.

old / nice / interesting   quickly / badly / suddenly
(adjectives and adverbs)

153 Complete the story about Jane's visit to China. Use the adjectives from the box + a suitable noun.

big	busy	delicious	difficult	famous	friendly	hot	~~long~~	old

Yesterday, Jane Greenwood flew back to London from China. It was a very (1) ..... long flight ..... –
12 hours – and she feels tired today.

   Jane was on holiday in China. She stayed in an (2) .... Three hundred
years ago an emperor built it. The only problem was that there was no (3) ....
in the rooms, so everybody had cold showers. She visited many (4) .... – for
example, The Great Wall of China. She ate some (5) .... Her favourite was
egg fried rice. She met a lot of very (6) .... Jane can't speak Chinese, so
they spoke to her in English. She tried a few words in Chinese, but people said it is a
(7) .... to learn.

   A lot of things in China surprised Jane. For example, the (8) .... There
were hundreds and hundreds of cars and bicycles on the roads all day and all night. There was
never a quiet moment.

   Jane wants to go back to China next year. She knows it's a (9) .... and she
only saw a small part of it.

154 Which is right?

MUM:	You were late home last night, Francesca.
FRANCESCA:	I know, I went to Javier's party, and afterwards I walked home.
MUM:	Didn't Joe offer to drive you home?
FRANCESCA:	Yes, but I think he drives (1) <u>dangerously</u> / ~~dangerous~~, so I said 'no'.
MUM:	Well, you look (2) <u>happily / happy</u> today. Was it a (3) <u>good / well</u> party?
FRANCESCA:	Yeah, great. Martin was there and he had his guitar with him. He plays really (4) <u>good / well</u>.
MUM:	I didn't know he was (5) <u>good / well</u> on the guitar.
FRANCESCA:	He plays flamenco music (6) <u>brilliant / brilliantly</u>. And Carmen was there and she's a (7) <u>fantastic / fantastically</u> dancer. She taught us how to do a bit of flamenco dancing. She explained really (8) <u>careful / carefully</u> and everybody did quite (9) <u>good / well</u>.
MUM:	Sounds fun. Would you like something to eat? I'm doing some bacon and eggs.
FRANCESCA:	Oh yes, please. It smells (10) <u>delicious / deliciously</u>.
MUM:	What have you got to do today?
FRANCESCA:	Well, we've got a maths exam next week and I did really (11) <u>badly / bad</u> in the last one, so I've got to work (12) <u>hard / hardly</u> today.
MUM:	OK, well eat this (13) <u>quick / quickly</u>, and get started.

older (than)   the oldest   not as old as
(comparatives and superlatives)

Complete this comparison between the USA and Australia. Write one word only in each space.

The USA has a much (1) ....*bigger*.... population (2) .... Australia, and American cities are (3) .... crowded than Australian ones.

There are not (4) .... many mountains in Australia (5) .... in the USA. Both countries have deserts and beautiful beaches. But America has (6) .... rivers than Australia.

The northern and central parts of the USA have much (7) .... snow in winter than anywhere in Australia and generally these two areas have a (8) .... winter than Australia does. Australia is in the southern hemisphere and doesn't have its winter at the same time (9) .... countries in the northern hemisphere.

Most people in these countries speak the same language (10) .... each other – English – but the accents are very different. Some people say that the Australians are warmer and (11) .... friendly (12) .... the Americans, but I don't see any difference.

Now write some sentences comparing your country with another country that you know. Use the comparison of the USA and Australia to help you. Write about:

- the geography (rivers, mountains etc.)
- the weather (hot, wet, dry, cold etc.)
- the people (language, character etc.)

....
....
....
....
....
....

Albert is thinking about life today and life 50 years ago. Complete his sentences. Use the comparative (**faster, harder,** etc.) or **not as ... as.**

1 (cars / fast)   *Cars are faster than they were.*
2 (children / more things)   *Children have got more things than they had.*
3 (people / work / hard)   *People don't work as hard as they did.*
4 (life / expensive)   ....
5 (people / not / friendly)   ....
6 (films / violent)   ....
7 (people / live / long)   ....
8 (houses / good)   ....
9 (families / not big)   ....
10 (children / freedom)   ....
11 (people / eat / good food) ....

157 | Put the alternatives into the correct order, starting with the largest, most common etc.

1 A Tiananmen Square, Beijing
   B Trafalgar Square, London
   C Times Square, New York

large square

Answer: _A, B, C_
Tiananmen Square is the largest
square and Trafalgar Square is
larger than Times Square.

2 A the cobra
   B the python
   C the rattlesnake

long snake

Answer: ....
....
....

A  B C

3 A Scotland
   B Antarctica
   C France

cold place

Answer: ....
....
....

4 A the cheetah
   B the mouse
   C the lion

fast animal

Answer: ....
....
....

A  B  C

5 A into
   B at
   C of

common
preposition
in English

Answer: ....
....
....

6 A the Great White Shark
   B the cockroach
   C the scorpion

dangerous
creature

Answer: ....
....
....

A 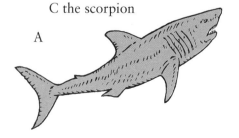 B  C

Terry is asking you some questions about your life. Write his questions. Use the superlative + the present perfect (**the most beautiful ... you've ever seen** etc.). Answer the questions in your own words.

1 TERRY: What / good / holiday / you / ever have?
            What's the best holiday you've ever had?
   YOU: _My holiday in Greece last year._
2 TERRY: Who / interesting person / you / ever meet?

   YOU:
3 TERRY: What / frightening experience / you / ever have?

   YOU:
4 TERRY: What / bad film / you / ever see?

   YOU:
5 TERRY: What / expensive thing / you / ever buy?

   YOU:
6 TERRY: What / unusual food / you / ever eat?

   YOU:
7 TERRY: Which / large city / you / ever visit?

   YOU:

There are mistakes in ten of these sentences. Correct the sentences where necessary. Write 'OK' if the sentence is already correct.

1 He got up <u>more early</u> than she did.   _He got up earlier than she did._
2 Jo lives much more far away now.
3 My mum is the same age like my dad.
4 I paid less than you for the ticket.
5 This is the older house in the city.
6 Traffic in the city is more bad in the evenings.
7 This dictionary is best I've ever had.
8 Paul isn't as lazy than he seems.
9 Is there a better hotel in town?
10 Meg is the more intelligent person in her family.
11 It's not as warmer as it was yesterday.
12 This is the comfortablest chair in the room.

160 Put the word **enough** in the correct place.

1 Is your English good for a translator's job? .....your English good enough.....
2 Have you got money to pay for the tickets? ....
3 Have you got information to answer the question? ....
4 Has he worked hard to pass his exams? ....
5 Are there plates for everyone? ....
6 Is your tea sweet or would you like some more sugar? ....

161 Complete the sentences. Use the words from the box + **enough** + **to** ... (**to do**, **to drive** etc.).

| money | ~~old~~ | sharp | time | warm | well |

1 Mary is 14 years old. She isn't ......old enough to drive...... a car.
2 I can't use this knife. It's not .... the meat.
3 Oh dear! I haven't got .... Pete a birthday present. Can you lend me some?
4 You should stay in bed. You don't look .... to Tina's party.
5 That was a horrible test. Did you have .... all the questions?
6 It's only 13 degrees. It's not .... tennis outside.

162 Complete the sentences. Use **too** + adjective or **too much / too many** + noun.

1 Sara didn't buy the coat because it ......was too expensive.. .
2 Carl felt ill last night because he ....
3 Jack doesn't use his bicycle in town because there ....
4 I don't like going shopping in the market because there ....
5 You shouldn't go to the beach at midday because it ....
6 Amir didn't sleep very well last night because he ....

Marco lives in an old city. It's very popular with tourists. He doesn't like it. Look at what Marco doesn't like about the city and complete the sentences. Use **too** or **enough**.

1　There _are too many cars._
2　The _streets are not wide enough._ **or**
　　The streets are too narrow.
3　There ....
4　There ....
5　The .... **or**
　　..
6　There ....
7　There ....

> 1　cars – a lot
> 2　streets – very narrow
> 3　cinemas – only 2
> 4　noise and dirt – a lot
> 5　the parks – very small
> 6　the evenings – very few things to do
> 7　tourists – a lot

What about the place where you live? Are there some things you don't like? Use **too** and **enough** to write about your city / town / village.

....

....

....

When are you allowed to do certain things?

In Britain, at the age of:
　5　You start primary school.
　12　You can buy a pet (e.g. a dog or a cat).
　13　You can work for two hours a day.
　16　You can leave school.
　　　You can get married with your parents' permission.
　17　You can drive a car.
　18　You can vote.

Use the information above to say whether these people are old enough. Use **too** and **enough**.

1　John is only 3 years old, but he wants to go to school. Can he?
　No, he's too young to go to school. **or** _He's not old enough to go to school._
2　My daughter is 14. Can she work in a shop after school?
　Yes, she's old enough to work for two hours a day.
3　Can Jane and Tom get married? They're 15.
　..
4　Can Peter start driving lessons? He's 17.
　..
5　Barbara's 10 and she wants to buy a dog with her own money. Can she?
　..
6　Shaun is 16 and fed up with school. Can he leave?
　..
7　Anna is 17 and very interested in politics. Can she vote?
　..

165 Write the sentences with **often, still, also** etc.

1 Rachel is late for school.
  (often) _Rachel is often late for school._

2 Maria goes to bed before midnight.
  (rarely) ....

3 I've got lots of friends, but they are on holiday at the moment.
  (all) ....

4 I like chocolate.
  (very much) ....

5 When do you do your homework?
  (usually) ....

6 I can remember my car registration number.
  (never) ....

7 Carmen always arrives late from work.
  (home) ....

8 Clare is a good piano player. She's learning to play the guitar.
  (also) ....

9 John and Steve? They are living in Brazil now.
  (both) ....

10 José finished his exams.
  (yesterday) ....

166 Complete the sentences. Use **still** (+ positive verbs) and **yet** (+ negative verbs).

1 TEACHER: OK everyone. Stop now. Please give me your test papers.
  STUDENT: Sorry, I _haven't finished yet_ . (finish) _I'm still writing_ . (write)

2 SALLY: Come, on we're going to be late.
  MARK: I .... my keys. (look for)
    I .... (find them)

3 Dear Sue
  The weather continues to be wet. It .... (rain)
  We .... (see the sun)

4 *(on the phone)*
  SUE: You sound very sleepy.
  KAREN: Yes, I .... (get up)
    I .... in bed. (be)

5 DAVE: Are you and Tony friends again?
  IAN: No. He .... (apologise)
    I .... with him. (be angry)

6 SAM: What car have you got at the moment?
  TONY: I .... my old Toyota. (drive)
    I .... (buy a new car)

and but or so because when ...

Read about Jane's Friday morning. Complete the sentences with **and**, **but**, **or**, **so** or **because**.

'On Friday morning I woke up late (1) ......because...... I'd forgotten to set the alarm clock the night before. I jumped out of bed (2) ......and...... got dressed quickly. I wanted to wash my hair, (3) .... I didn't have enough time to do that (4) .... have breakfast too. Big decision! Shall I wash my hair (5) .... have breakfast? Breakfast won. I needed some toast and coffee, (6) .... unfortunately the toaster burnt the bread, (7) .... I just drank the coffee.

I ran out of the house to catch the bus. It was raining hard (8) .... I didn't have my umbrella with me, (9) .... I got wet. I had to wait at the bus stop for 20 minutes (10) .... no bus arrived. Then I saw a taxi coming down the road, (11) .... I put up my arm to catch the driver's attention. Unfortunately, he didn't see me and drove past. I now had the choice of walking to work in the rain, waiting for another taxi (12) .... going home. I went home (13) .... rang my office. "I'm really sorry, I can't come in today (14) .... I've got a terrible cold." And I stayed in bed all day.'

Complete the conversations. Use any other words that are necessary.

1 LISA: How long has Anne worked at Harrods?

  ALLY: She started there ...after she finished college... . (after / finish college)

2 STEVE: I thought Joe lived in Manchester.

  SUE: He used to. ...Before he got married..., he lived there. (before / get married)

3 HELEN: Ooh! Are these flowers for me?

  JACK: Yes, they arrived .... (while / at work)

4 DAN: What did the doctor say, Mum?

  MUM: You mustn't go back to school .... (until / better)

5 SAM: Dad, Dad. Come and play football with me.

  DAD: Sam, be quiet. Don't talk to me ....
    (when / speak on phone)

6 ALAN: ...., I'm going to travel for six months.
    (when / finish college)

  WILL: Can I come with you?

7 ADAM: Oh, Maria, you're completely wet!

  MARIA: I know. ...., it started raining hard.
    (while / walk home)

8 MARK: OK, we're ready. Let's go.

  LUCY: Hang on. I must make sure the cat is outside ....
    (before / leave the house)

9 JILL: I can't believe that Clare's writing a book! I've never even seen her reading one.

  RICHARD: I know! ...., I thought it was a joke.
    (when / hear the news)

10 JENNY: Oh, no! I've broken my lovely blue vase.

  MIKE: Don't worry. I'll get you another one .... tomorrow.
    (when / in town)

169 Jill and Tina are waiting at the bus stop. They're on their way to the cinema. Complete their story. Use the end of the previous sentence to make the beginning of the next sentence.

SUE: Oh dear, what's happened to the bus? Why hasn't it come?

TINA: If (1) _the bus doesn't come_ soon, we'll be late.

SUE: If (2) .... late, we'll miss the beginning of the film.

TINA: If (3) .... the film, we won't understand the story.

SUE: If (4) .... the story, we'll be bored.

TINA: If (5) ...., we'll probably fall asleep.

SUE: If (6) ...., we'll miss the end of the film.

TINA: Let's not go to the cinema.

170 There is a mistake in each of these sentences. One verb is right and the other is wrong. Correct the verbs that are wrong.

1 If I will see Anne, I won't ask her about the exam. ...... see ......
2 I haven't got a bike. If I have one, I would lend it to you. ....
3 Barbara's in bed with a fever. She would be here with you
  if she wouldn't be ill. ....
4 All the plants in the garden will die if it won't rain soon. ....
5 What would you do if you would find a lot of money in the street? ....
6 Ben doesn't get up early enough to catch the 6.30 train.
  If he would get up earlier, he wouldn't be late. ....
7 If I ask Tony for the answer, I know he doesn't tell me. ....

171 What do you say in the following situations? Make sentences with the words.

1 Paul has asked you to go to a jazz concert. You don't like jazz, so you're not going with him.
  (I / go / with you / if I / like / jazz) _I'd go with you if I liked jazz._
2 You're in a restaurant with your sister. She's got some peas on her plate. You know she doesn't like them, but you do!
  (If you / not / want / your / peas / I / eat / them) _If you don't want your peas, I'll eat them._
3 You want to go on holiday, but you're very busy at college at the moment.
  (If I / not / be / busy at college / I / go / on holiday) ....
4 You want to buy a new laptop. The one you're looking at is quite cheap, but it doesn't have any more memory than the one you've got.
  (If it / have / a bigger memory / I / buy / it) ....
5 Your brother is going to buy an old car in bad condition. You don't think it's a good idea.
  (I / not / buy it / if I / be / you) ....
6 You and Sarah are at the railway station, waiting for David. You are all going to Manchester. David is late and the train leaves in five minutes.
  (We / miss / the train / if he / not / arrive / soon) ....

a person (who) ...   a thing (that/which) ...
(relative clauses)

Make one sentence from two sentences. Use **who** or **which**.

1 James lives on an island. It is famous for its beautiful beaches.
James _lives on an island which is famous for its beautiful beaches_ .

2 There's a new chef in our canteen. He's very good at making desserts.
There's a new chef _in our canteen who's very good at making desserts_ .

3 A car crashed into mine. It was green.
The car _____ .

4 Where's the newspaper? It was on the table.
Where _____ ?

5 A backpack was left on the bus yesterday. It belongs to my sister.
The backpack _____ my sister.

6 I spoke to an assistant. She had long, dark hair.
I _____ .

7 Peter writes books. They are translated into many languages.
Peter _____ .

8 A lot of people went to last night's concert. They enjoyed it.
The people _____ .

Make one sentence from two sentences. Don't use **who**, **that** or **which**.

1 Gill is looking at a man. She thinks she knows him.
Gill thinks she knows _the man she's looking at_ .

2 I worked in a shop. It was called 'Bangles'.
The shop I _____ .

3 I was watching elephants on TV. They were playing in a river.
The elephants I _____ .

4 'Sally stayed with some friends.'   'What's their name?'
What's the name _____ ?

5 Kate went on holiday with some people. They live in the same street.
The people _____ .

6 I'm reading a book. It was written over 300 years ago.
The book _____ .

7 You were waiting for a train. Did it arrive?
Did the train _____ ?

8 Fiona's playing tennis with a man. Who is he?
Who's the _____ ?

174 Complete the sentences. Read the extra information first.

GUIDE: Ladies and gentlemen, this is the house (1) ___Michael Barnes was born in___ .

(Michael Barnes was born in this house.)

CLARE: Who's Michael Barnes?

ADAM: He's the man (2) ....

(Michael Barnes wrote over 100 books.)

CLARE: I've never heard of him!

ADAM: You have! You know that film (3) .... ?

(We went to see a film last week.)

Well, it was based on one of his books.

CLARE: Oh.

GUIDE: And now, if you look on your right, you can see Jane Carter's house.

CLARE: Why is that important?

ADAM: You must remember! Jane Carter is the woman

(4) ....

(I told you about Jane Carter.)

CLARE: Oh yes. She lived until she was 100.

ADAM: That's right. And do you remember the name of the institute

(5) .... ?

(The institute was started by Jane Carter.)

CLARE: The Fellcome Institute, wasn't it?

ADAM: Yes, and it was the Fellcome Institute

(6) ....

(The Fellcome Institute gave me the money to study in America.)

CLARE: I remember now. So, this is her house. Interesting.

GUIDE: And now, let's go into the main street and look at the statue of King Henry VIII.

CLARE: I know about him. He's the king (7) ....

(Henry VIII made tennis popular.)

ADAM: Did he? I thought you were going to say that he's the king

(8) ....

(He had six wives.)

CLARE: Well, let's go and see him, anyway.

at until before
(prepositions of time)

5 Complete the sentences. Choose words from the boxes.

at		night	22 November 1963	winter
on	+	midnight	Thursday morning	6.30 am
in		~~the evening~~	the weekend	1920

1 After working all day, John is too tired to go out ......*in the evening*...... .
2 Last night I went to bed ....
3 President Kennedy was shot ....
4 Our cat stays out .... and comes back in the morning.
5 Jill loves skiing, so she usually takes her holidays ....
6 My parents' alarm clock always rings ....
7 Clare's grandfather was born .... , so he's now a very old man.
8 I've had a busy week, so I'm going to stay at home ....
9 I have a lecture .... , so I can't meet you then, I'm afraid.

6 Complete the text with the words from the box. Use some words more than once.

after	at	before	for	from	in	on	since	until	to

The Channel Tunnel

The Channel Tunnel is 50 kilometres long and is between Britain and France. There are two tunnels for trains and one smaller service tunnel.

The tunnel was first talked about (1) ....*at*.... the beginning of the 19th century. This, of course, was (2) .... trains and cars were invented. (3) .... 1802, it was suggested that two tunnels could be built for carriages which would be pulled by horses. Fortunately, nothing happened. Then (4) .... the end of the 19th century, the English Channel Company started to build a tunnel. Engineers on both sides began digging (5) .... 1881. Technically, it was a success. (6) .... the first year, each side had dug almost two kilometres of tunnel. But digging stopped two years later because Britain and France were no longer political friends. (7) .... then (8) .... 1966, nothing more happened. (9) .... 1966, the Prime Ministers of Britain and France decided to try again, and (10) .... 20 years of talking, work

began (11) .... December 1987. The French and British tunnel workers 'met' (12) .... the 1st of December 1990. The engineers said the tunnel would be ready for opening (13) .... five years' time. In fact, it was two years late. It opened (14) .... May 1994. (15) .... that time, the channel tunnel trains have carried millions of passengers. It takes about three hours to travel between London and Paris, and during that time, the train is under the Channel (16) .... about 20 minutes.

177 Complete the story of Jess Brewer's life. Use the words from the box.

after	before	during	for	~~from~~	since	to/until	until	while

Jess Brewer was a pupil at her local school (1) .....*from*..... 1980 (2) .... 1993. (3) ....
her last year at school she learnt how to use computers, and this knowledge was very useful for
her later. (4) .... leaving school, she went to university and studied mathematics. She was
responsible for producing a student magazine (5) .... she was there. She stayed at
university (6) .... four years and then decided to travel (7) .... looking for a job.
She has been working as a computer programmer (8) .... she came back from her travels,
but she wants to go away again. She knows that she has to stay with the computer company
(9) .... she has enough money to go and do what she wants.

Jess is describing a normal day in her life. Complete her story with the words from the box.
Use some words more than once.

after	~~at~~	before	~~during~~	for	from	in	on	since	to	until	while

'I wake up (10) .....*at*..... about 7.30 (11) .....*during*..... the week, but much later (12) ....
Saturdays. (13) .... I wake up, I move very fast. In fact, I'm very good (14) .... the
mornings. I only need 20 minutes (15) .... the time my alarm clock rings (16) ....
the time I leave the house. I don't have breakfast at home; I have to wait (17) .... I arrive
at the office for a cup of coffee.
  I start work (18) .... 9 o'clock and work (19) .... four hours. (20) ....
lunchtime, I often sit in the park and read (21) .... I'm eating my sandwiches.
(22) .... going back to the office, I do some shopping. The afternoon passes very quickly. I
work (23) .... 6 o'clock and then I go home. I've been working for the same company
(24) .... 1999.
  (25) .... the evenings, I usually watch TV or maybe go out for dinner with some friends.
I don't go to bed late because I have to get up for work the next day. (26) .... weekends,
my routine is very different.

Now write a paragraph about a normal day in your life. Use the words from the box to help
you.

wake up / get up	breakfast	work / school	lunchtime	afternoon	evenings	bed

..... I usually wake up ....
....
....
....

in under through
(prepositions of place and movement)

3 Some customers in the supermarket can't find what they want. You are the assistant.
Complete the sentences.

CUSTOMER 1: I can't find the cereals.

YOU: They're ..*on*.. the left, ..*on*.. the bottom shelf, ..*below*.. the sugar.

CUSTOMER 2: Where's the rice, please?

YOU: It's .... the left, ... the top shelf, ... the pasta and the bread.

CUSTOMER 3: Where are the biscuits, please?

YOU: They're .... the right, ... shelf, ... the nuts.

CUSTOMER 4: Where's the water, please?

YOU: It's .... the right, ... shelf, ... the cola.

CUSTOMER 5: I can't find the tea.

YOU: It's .... the right, ... shelf, ... the cola.

CUSTOMER 6: And the cakes?

YOU: They're .... the cola, ... shelf, ... middle, ... the biscuits and the chocolate.

CUSTOMER 7: And the coffee?

YOU: ....
....

CUSTOMER 8: And the flour?

YOU: ....
....

179 Complete Leo's story using **to**, **in** or **at** if necessary. In one sentence, no preposition is necessary.

'I'm flying (1) ......*to*...... Italy on Sunday the 2nd of September, and the plane arrives (2) .... Rome airport at 11 o'clock at night. I'm staying (3) .... Rome (4) .... the Park Hotel for three days. Then, on Wednesday, I'm going (5) .... Bangkok for five days. I'll arrive (6) .... the Plaza Hotel (7) .... the centre of Bangkok late on Wednesday evening. On Saturday, I'm meeting a friend of mine (8) .... the hotel. He lives (9) .... the north of Thailand and is coming (10) .... Bangkok. We're going on holiday together.

 On Monday the 10th, we're taking a boat (11) .... one of the islands, Ko Samui. We're staying there for two weeks. It's going to be wonderful. On the 26th, we return (12) .... Bangkok. Early the next day, I fly back (13) .... England. I arrive (14) .... home in the middle of the night. A wonderful month for me!'

180 Look at the journey that Felix, the cat, made in Sue's garden. Complete the story with prepositions (**over**, **up**, **into**, **out of** etc.).

Felix jumped (1) ......*over*...... the wall and walked (2) ......*across*...... the grass. Then he went (3) .... the pond and (4) .... the path. He walked (5) .... Sue's chair and (6) .... the table. Suddenly, he jumped (7) .... the table and took the fish which was (8) .... Sue's plate. He jumped (9) .... the table with the fish. Then the dog, Rosie, came (10) .... the house and chased the cat. They both ran (11) .... the bushes and (12) .... the patio. Felix stopped suddenly, but Rosie fell (13) .... the pond. Felix looked at her and then jumped (14) .... the wall again, still holding the fish in his mouth.

good at (doing)   listen to
(prepositions before and after verbs)

1 Complete the second sentence in each pair so that it has the same meaning. Use a preposition (**to, at, with** etc.).

1 I always got the best mark in history at school.
I _was good at history at school_ . (good)

2 The apples you bought yesterday were green. These are red.
These apples .... (different)

3 Turn the TV off, please. It's rugby and I don't like it.
I .... (not interested)

4 Rain, rain, rain! I'd like some sunshine for a change.
I .... (fed up)

5 Charlie doesn't like storms. They frighten him.
Charlie .... (afraid)

6 Stuart can't cook. A boiled egg is too difficult for him!
Stuart .... (not very good)

7 Jess always helps her elderly neighbours.
Jess .... (nice)

8 You can't move in my grandmother's sitting room. She's got a lot of furniture.
My grandmother's sitting room .... (full)

9 What's the matter? Why are you shouting at Liz?
Why .... ? (angry)

2 Complete the letter. Use a preposition + verb.

Dear Lynne,
Thanks (1) _for sending_ (send) me the photos of John. I'm sorry
(2) .... (not / write) before, but I've been very busy
at work. In fact, I'm thinking (3) .... (leave). I'm just
not interested (4) .... (sell) cars any more. I liked
the job at first, but now I'm fed up (5) .... (say)
the same things to everyone – you know, how wonderful the cars are,
etc. Do you think I should look for a new job? It's a big decision to
take. I'm a bit afraid (6) .... (be) unemployed. I know
I'm good (7) .... (sell) things, but I really need a
change. What do you think I should do?
Hope to hear from you soon.

Love,
Mark

183 Read this interview between a police officer and Tina Bledlow, who saw a bank robbery yesterday. Write a preposition where necessary. There is no preposition in one sentence.

OFFICER: Can you tell us what you saw?

TINA: Well, Joe and I were standing opposite the bank, waiting (1) ....._for_..... a bus. I was talking (2) .... Joe (3) .... the film we were going to see. I know he wasn't really listening (4) .... me because he was looking (5) .... a car which was parked across the road.

OFFICER: What kind of car was it?

TINA: A blue Mercedes, I think. Anyway, I decided to call (6) .... my friend, Naomi. I wanted to thank her (7) .... the present she gave me for my birthday on Saturday. And I needed to ask her (8) .... another friend's mobile number.

OFFICER: And what was Joe doing while you were speaking (9) .... your friend?

TINA: Reading a holiday brochure. We're planning to go away next month. To be honest, I think he was fed up (10) .... listening to me on the phone.

OFFICER: And did you see the two women coming out of the bank, and getting into the car?

TINA: Yes, I remember thinking that they looked very well-dressed. Joe was looking (11) .... them, too.

OFFICER: We'd like to interview Joe. We've looked (12) .... him at his address, but he wasn't there. We found this mobile at his apartment. Do you know if it belongs (13) .... him?

TINA: Yes, it's his.

OFFICER: Tina, we think that Joe knows something about the bank robbery. Now, tell us …

4 Complete the sentences with **up**, **off**, **in** etc.

1 Hurry ___up___ , Patti. The plane takes ___off___ in ten minutes.

2 Jane was asleep on the bus. Suddenly, the bus driver said, 'Wake _____ ! This is your stop.' Jane quickly got _____ and the bus drove _____ .

3 A young boy ran out of the sweet shop and rode _____ on his bike. Two seconds later, the shop assistant came out and shouted, 'Come _____ ! You haven't paid!'

4 Be careful! There's an old woman trying to cross the road. I think you're driving too fast. Slow _____ a bit, please.

5 If you've finished Exercise 6, turn _____ and carry _____ . Exercises 7 and 8 are on page 5.

6 SUE: Can I speak to Bob, please?

    MEG: Sorry, I can't hear you. Can you speak _____ ?

    SUE: Can I speak to Bob, please.

    MEG: Yes, hold _____ a minute. He's in the kitchen, washing _____ . I'll call him. BOB!

7 One cold night last winter my car broke _____ . I went to a house and asked for help. The man there was very kind and said, 'Come _____ and keep warm.'

5 Complete the sentences with a verb + **on**, **off**, **up** etc.

1 You're in a clothes shop. You want to buy some jeans, but first you want to see if they're the right size. What do you ask the shop assistant?

Can I ___try these jeans on___ , please?

2 It's dark in the room. You need some light. What do you ask?

Could you _____ , please?

3 Your father can't read the newspaper because he isn't wearing his glasses. What do you tell him to do?

_____ , Dad.

4 You borrow some money from a friend. You promise to return it tomorrow. What do you say?

I'll _____ tomorrow.

5 Your grandmother has dropped a magazine on the floor and she can't get it. What does she ask you?

Could you _____ for me, please?

6 Your sister's playing her music very loudly. You don't mind, but you don't want it so loud. What do you ask her?

Could you _____ a bit, please?

7 You're in the sitting room and the TV is on. Your mother comes in and asks if you're watching it. What do you say?

No, not really. You can _____ .

8 You've found some very old tomatoes in the fridge. What do you ask?

Do you want these tomatoes or shall I _____ ?

Key

In many of these answers you can use the full form of the verb (*I am*, *he has* etc.) or the short form of the verb (*I'm*, *she's* etc.)

1

3 'm/am
4 is
5 'm not/am not
6 'm not/am not
7 is
8 isn't/is not
9 's/is
10 are
11 aren't/are not
12 's/is
13 's/is

Example answer:
His name is Steve.
He's 45 years old.
He's an engineer.
He's interested in cars.
He isn't at work today
  because he's sick.

2

2 Where are you ... ?
3 How ... are you?
4 What colour are your ... ?
5 What's your ... ?
6 What are you ... ?
7 Who's your ... ?
8 Why are you ... ?

3

2 Russia aren't islands.
3 Peas are green.
   Carrots and onions aren't green.
4 Elephants and whales are big (animals).
   Cats aren't big (animals).
5 Gold is expensive.
   Milk and ice-cream aren't expensive.
6 *Example answers:*
   I'm interested in sport.
   I'm not interested in politics and music.

4

2 How old is he?
3 Is ... your ... ?
4 Who's that?
5 How old is she?
6 Is that ... ?
7 What's his name?
8 Are those ... ?

5

There are a lot more than ten possible sentences in this exercise. Example answers:
3 Are your parents old?
4 I'm/am an engineer.
5 How old is Anna?
6 Jim's book isn't expensive.
7 Where's/is Anna?
8 Your parents aren't at work.
9 How are your parents?
10 I'm/am not 18.

6

+ -ing
helping
laughing
listening
playing
starting
wearing
working
n → nn, t → tt etc.
digging
forgetting
putting
robbing
stopping
swimming
winning
e → ing
coming
dancing
deciding
having
living
making
writing
ie → ying
lying
tying

7

2 'm lying / am lying
3 am watching *or* watching
4 are swimming
5 aren't swimming
6 're standing / are standing
7 are watching *or* watching
8 are playing
9 isn't lying
10 's sitting / is sitting
11 's wearing / is wearing
12 is eating *or* eating

8

2 Sam and Eric aren't playing with a ball.
   They're playing with a train.
3 They aren't wearing sunglasses.
   They're wearing hats.
4 Pam isn't cooking chicken.
   She's cooking fish.
5 She isn't laughing.
   She's crying.
6 Jo isn't standing with her mother.
   She's lying on the grass.
7 She isn't eating an orange.
   She's eating a banana.
8 Fred, the dog, isn't lying on the grass asleep.
   He's playing with a ball.

9

2 Where are you sitting?
3 Why are you laughing?
4 What are you watching?
5 Are you enjoying (it)?
6 Is he cooking (dinner)?
7 Who's he talking (to)?
8 Are they talking (to James)?
9 What are they making?

10

2 She doesn't drive a car.
   She rides (a bike).
3 She doesn't work in an office.
   She stays (at home).
4 She doesn't have lunch in a restaurant.
   She makes (lunch at home).
5 She doesn't like cats.
   She prefers (dogs).
6 She doesn't play computer games.
   She watches (TV).

11

2 sleeps
3 has
4 holds
5 doesn't move
6 takes
7 costs

8 don't pay
9 don't want
10 doesn't work

12

2 <u>Do you go</u> to the office every day?
3 My car <u>doesn't work</u> when it <u>is</u> cold.
4 What time <u>does the film start</u>?
5 <u>How many eggs do you want</u> for breakfast?
6 *OK*
7 What <u>does your father do</u>?
8 I <u>don't write</u> many letters. I usually use email.
9 What <u>does</u> Sue usually have for lunch?
10 *OK*
11 Charlie <u>plays</u> tennis, but he doesn't enjoy it.

13

2 St John's Hospital
3 10 o'clock
4 6 o'clock
5 bus
6 20 children
7 many times
8 wakes the children up
9 gives them breakfast
10 very tired

12 do you work
13 do you start work
14 do you finish
15 do you go to work
16 children do you have in your section
17 do you look at the children
18 does the day nurse arrive
19 does she do
20 do you usually feel

14

2 Do you go
3 How do you get/travel
4 How much does it cost
5 Where do you (usually) sit
6 What/Which kind of films do you like
7 What's your favourite
8 Do you eat/buy

10 walks
11 lives
12 costs
13 sits
14 likes
15 is
16 doesn't eat
17 has/buys/drinks

(Use the paragraph about Paula to help you with your answer.)

15

2 I'm writing
3 I hate
4 Do you remember
5 he's lying
6 keeping
7 he sleeps
8 he doesn't catch
9 are watching
10 They like
11 They aren't laughing
12 I work
13 I don't want
14 are you doing
15 you're sitting
18 the sun's shining

16

Example answer:
Every day I get up at 7 o'clock and clean my teeth. I go for a run and then I have a shower.
At the moment I'm sitting in my room and I'm doing this exercise. I'm holding a cup of coffee in my left hand and I'm thinking about my lunch.

17

2 What do you do?
   What are you doing?
3 When do you usually finish work?
   Why are you leaving now?
4 What's John doing?
   Does he read a lot?
5 Why are the children running?
   What time do they start school?

18

3 's raining

4 's reading
5 aren't watching
6 do you get up
7 Does Sandra eat
8 are you smiling
9 don't understand

19

2 Do you read a newspaper every day?
   Yes, I do. / No, I don't.
3 Does it rain much in your country?   Yes, it does. / No, it doesn't.
4 Do you usually do your homework on a computer? Yes, I do. / No, I don't.
5 Are you having a drink now?
   Yes, I am. / No, I'm not.
6 Do you drink coffee for breakfast every day?
   Yes, I do. / No, I don't.
7 Are you working at the moment?
   Yes, I am. / No, I'm not.
8 Do students eat lunch at school in your country?
   Yes, they do. /
   No, they don't.

20

2 's/has got
3 hasn't got
4 have got
5 's/has got
6 's/has got
7 hasn't got
8 's/has got
9 's/has got
10 's/has got
11 haven't got

Example answers:
I've got blue eyes. I haven't got a brother.
My mother has got a kind face. She hasn't got a lot of money.
Our neighbours haven't got a dog. They've got a garden.
My teacher has got a digital camera. She hasn't got a car.
My best friend has got a problem. She hasn't got a job.

21

2 have they got
3 has it got
4 Has he got
5 Have they got
6 Has she got
7 Have you got

22

2 He was
3 It was
4 They were
5 It was
6 We were
7 They were
8 I was

23

Example answers:
2 I was in the city centre
3 I was at the cinema
4 I was at the sports centre
5 I was in bed
6 I was in a restaurant
7 I was in the park

24

2 Was it difficult … it wasn't
3 Was it fast … it was
4 Were they expensive … they weren't
5 Were you nervous … I wasn't
6 Was she ill … she was

25

2 had lunch
3 went to an art exhibition
4 met Chris
5 didn't go to the Tango Club
6 bought a birthday present
7 had a picnic by the river
8 didn't take a boat cruise
9 made dinner in Sarah's apartment
10 caught the late flight home

Example answer:
On Friday morning I got up at eight o'clock and had breakfast. I went to work as usual. At one o'clock I had lunch with two of my colleagues. In the afternoon I didn't go to work. I went to the dentist. I had an appointment at half past two. After my appointment, I went shopping. I bought some jeans and two T-shirts. In the evening I went to the cinema with some friends, but I didn't enjoy the film very much.

26

Did you go to school?
Did you have a big lunch?
Did you have a history lesson?
Did you play football?
Did you spend any money?
Did you visit your grandmother?
Did you watch any TV?

27

2 didn't have
3 won
4 taught
5 was
6 left
7 studied
8 wasn't
9 wore
10 sang
11 made
12 went
13 spent
14 met
15 married
16 had
17 weren't
18 died

28

2 When did he win a school singing competition?
3 How did he learn to play the guitar?
4 Why did his family move to Memphis?
5 When did he leave school?
6 Did he work? *or* Did he have a job?
7 Why did he study at night school?
8 What did people love (about him)?
9 How many movies did he make?
10 How long was he in the army? *or* … did he stay in the army?
11 Who did he marry?
12 Did they have any children? *or* … have a child?
13 When did he die?

29

2 spent/had
3 was
4 saw/visited
5 climbed/went
6 was
7 were
8 took/caught
9 walked/went
10 weren't
11 went
12 thought
13 didn't like / didn't enjoy
14 was

(Use the postcard from Elena to help you with your answer.)

30

2 Sam was climbing a tree in the park.
3 Sam's dogs were running in the park. *or* … were playing in the park.
4 Lynn was lying on the grass in the park.
5 Mrs Drake was going into the baker's.
6 Philip was sitting in the garden.
7 Mike and Tim were waiting at the bus stop.
8 Felix was sleeping on a/the car.
9 Paul was getting into a/the/his car.

Example answers:
10 At 10.30 in the morning I was sitting in my office.
11 At 12.30 I was having lunch.
12 At 6.15 in the evening I was writing an email.
13 At 8.30 in the evening I was cooking the dinner.
14 At midnight I was sleeping.

31

1 Did you see … was reading
2 telephoned … was sitting … drinking … Was … was working … did you go … went
3 broke … was washing … were … dropped
4 Did you think … was … didn't write … was dreaming
5 was … happened … was raining … weren't going … Were … broke … cut
6 wasn't talking … were you talking

32

2 Where was Joan Turner?
3 What was Mrs Jones doing?
4 Where was Mrs Walters going?
5 Were the robbers carrying guns?
6 Where was the big car waiting?
7 Was the driver a man or a woman?
8 Did you see a man on the corner?
9 Were some men repairing the road?
10 Was anyone waiting at the bus stop?
11 Did you phone the police?

13 was in the baker's
14 was walking along the street
15 was going into the baker's
16 were carrying
17 was waiting opposite the bank
18 was a woman
19 was standing
20 were repairing
21 were waiting
22 phoned

33

3 What does he do?
4 What does he study?
5 What does he like?
6 Where did he go for his last holiday?

7 Where did he stay?
8 What did he do on holiday?

Example answer:
Jill is 29 and she lives in Dublin. She's a computer programmer and she studied mathematics at university. She likes travelling, swimming and chocolate. Last year she went to Thailand for one month with friends. She stayed in a hotel by the sea and she did lots of water sports.

(Use the paragraphs about Marco and Jill to help you with your answer.)

34

3 *OK*
4 usually go
5 didn't have
6 are you looking
7 're/are wearing
8 bought
9 is Tim doing
10 fell
11 *OK*
12 Did he hurt
13 woke
14 didn't watch
15 don't usually watch
16 went
17 *OK*
18 *OK*

35

2 was
3 went
4 was sitting
5 walked
6 saw
7 was
8 was
9 is
10 made
11 were
12 had
13 did it happen
14 were riding
15 stopped
16 fell
17 broke
18 talk
19 Do you ride
20 stopped

21 moved
22 do you do
23 likes
24 swims
25 love
26 'm making
27 's swimming

36

2 hasn't heard
3 've lost
4 've (already) bought
5 hasn't got
6 have (you) taken
7 've (never) tried
8 has (he) invited
9 has written
10 Has (he) lost
11 've broken
12 haven't seen

37

2 Have you ever had … Have you ever broken
3 Have you ever eaten
4 Have you ever travelled
5 Have you ever lost
6 Have you ever slept
7 Have you ever climbed

Two of the following:
He has broken his leg (twice).
He has travelled in a canoe.
He has slept outside.
He has climbed a high mountain.
And the following:
He has never eaten crocodile.
He has never lost his way.
Example answers:
I've broken my arm once.
I've never slept outside.

38

2 have (they) gone
have (they) been
3 have(n't) been
4 's gone
5 's gone … 's (already) been

39

2 have done
3 's/has travelled *or* been
4 's/has met *or* seen
5 's/has made *or* earned *or* won
6 's/has (already) written

7 's/has ridden
8 's/has (just) sold *or* sent
9 've/have played
10 've/have (never) been

40

2 How long have you been married to Paul?   For
3 How long have you had a (new) dog?   Since
4 How long have you worked as a hairdresser?   Since
5 How long has Paul been a train driver?   For
6 How long have your parents lived with you?   For
7 How long has your mother looked after the baby?   Since
8 How long has your father been ill?   Since

41

Example answers:
3 3 years ago
4 for three years *or* since 2003
5 10 years ago
6 since Monday *or* for three days
7 5 years ago … 2 years ago
8 since the summer *or* for a month

42

2 've been
3 've been waiting
4 's been
5 's had
6 's been shining
7 went
8 's lived *or* 's been living
9 got married
10 's known

43

2 John's been talking for 20 minutes.
3 They've been walking for six hours.
4 You've been watching TV since 9 o'clock this morning.
5 Laura's been feeling sick since lunchtime.
6 Fred's been travelling for two days / since June 28th.

7 It's been raining for 12 hours.

44

2 When did John lose his job?
3 How long has Ricardo had a cat?
4 What time did you finish work last night?
5 When was the last time you had a holiday?
6 How long did you watch TV last night?
7 When did Chris go out?
8 How long has your father been in hospital?

45

2 I've been here since last year.
3 *OK*
4 She was a photographer five years ago.
5 James and I met last March.
6 *OK*
7 John has been looking for a new job since last month.
8 Did you speak to your parents last night?
9 I've played the guitar since I was a child.
10 What did you do last night?

46

2 B		5 A	
3 A		6 A	
4 B			

47

2 has Jane/she had her computer
3 has been a politician for
4 has worked here *or* has been working here
5 haven't finished it/my homework
6 met his best friend, Ahmed,
7 have had flu for
8 has been interested in music

48

3 reached
4 have just started
5 did (they) spend
6 took
7 arrived
8 has been
9 said
10 have worked / have been working
11 has been
12 won
13 has won
14 was
15 scored
16 has been
17 left
18 have had
19 was

49

2 've lost … did (you last) see … left
3 bought … has (he) had
4 haven't finished … started
5 Did (you) see … Have (you ever) seen … 've also touched … was … was
6 's crashed … has (she) done

50

2 have you worked / have you been working
3 Do you like
4 was
5 are you looking
6 is
7 Has it gone/disappeared

51

2 was
3 watched
4 ate
5 had
6 enjoyed
7 'm writing
8 'm sitting
9 had
10 was
11 've been
12 came
13 have (got)
14 was
15 Do you like
16 's practising
17 've just sent

18 did you find *or* have you found
19 left
20 's sitting

52

1 time you spent with me very much. We had some good fun.
2 You left a big box of chocolates for my parents. Thank you. We've just finished them – they were delicious.
3 And thank you also for the CDs. They arrived yesterday. I haven't played all of them yet. At the moment I'm listening to 'Paradise Rock'. It's very good.
4 My mother found your photo album the day you left. I sent it back two weeks ago. Have you received it yet?
5 Do you remember Steve? We met him at Sue's party. Well, he came to my house last week. He asked for your address, so I gave it to him. I hope that's OK. He's in California now on business.
6 I'm looking out of the window at the moment. The sun's shining and it's a beautiful warm day. In fact, it has been sunny every day since you went back to San Francisco. Honestly!
7 The CD has just finished. Tell your brother I love his music. Does he want a publicity agent in London?

(Use exercise 51 to help you with your answer.)

53

Down	Across
1 chosen	5 read
2 written	6 bought
3 made	8 grown
4 found	9 spoken
7 thought	10 forgotten
10 felt	12 held
11 shot	13 taken
	14 built

54

2 How many languages are spoken in the world?
3 Where is coffee grown?
4 What is the country of Siam now called?
6 When was the first photograph taken?
7 Where were CDs first made?
8 When was the Taj Mahal built?
9 Where was John Lennon shot?

55

3 is locked
4 are checked
5 is being made
6 are being put
7 isn't exported
8 is washed
9 is allowed
10 is being served

56

what has been done
The lamp has been repaired.
The glass has been broken.
The lights have been switched/turned off.
The window has been closed.
what hasn't been done
The computer hasn't been switched off.
The chairs haven't been repaired.

57

3 was taken
4 caused
5 were covered
6 left
7 walked
8 are being repaired
9 has disappeared
10 have (just) been removed
11 have (just) heard
12 blew
13 is waiting
14 was
15 was sent
16 kicked
17 was hurt
18 crashed
19 was carried
20 played
21 is being taken

22 thinks
23 is happening
24 are being given

Example answers:
Bank robbery: €6 million taken
Thieves entered a bank in Bergamo yesterday and took €6 million. Six members of staff were locked in a room, but no-one was hurt. Police are now looking for a white van which was used to take away the money.

Dog attacks man outside supermarket
A man was attacked by a dog outside the Laftis supermarket yesterday afternoon. He was bitten on the arms and legs. The man was taken to hospital, but he has now been released.

Local woman wins lottery
A 55-year-old woman has won £3 million in the lottery. Jane Smith, a shop assisstant from Brighton, was told the news on Sunday morning.

Car hits actor on bike
The actor James Grady was hit by a car yesterday afternoon while he was cycling with friends. An ambulance was called and Grady was taken to hospital. The driver of the car was later arrested for dangerous driving.

58

2 has
3 was
4 doesn't
5 haven't
6 is
7 were
8 weren't
9 are
10 didn't

59

3 gave … forgot
4 found … left
5 showed … taken
6 escaped … caught
7 thought … done

8 wore … given
9 learnt/learned … fell … swum
10 felt … went … slept

60
2 have you
3 Did you
4 Was it
5 did you
6 Have you
7 was it
8 Does it *or* Do you
9 Do you
10 Has he

12 bought
13 had
14 got
15 chose
16 read
17 made
18 learnt
19 took
20 put
21 sent
22 used
23 shown

61
2 'm having
3 is coming
4 is getting married
5 are going
6 'm driving
7 does (the meeting) start
8 'm talking
9 leaves/goes/is

62
Example answers:
2 I'm going to the cinema.
3 I'm having lunch with my sister.
4 I'm playing football.
5 I'm working on Sunday.

63
3 When does the check-in desk open?
4 How are we travelling to the airport?
5 Where are we meeting Jane?
6 Where are we staying for the first night?

7 What time does the flight land?
8 Who's meeting us at the airport in Beijing?

Example answer:
We're meeting at 7 a.m. and the check-in desk opens at quarter past seven. We're going to the airport by train and we're meeting Jane at the station. We're staying at the Plaza Hotel in Beijing for the first night. The flight lands at 4 o'clock in the afternoon and someone from the hotel is meeting us.

64
2 What are you going to buy for Paul's birthday?
Is he going to have a party?
3 Are you going to buy a new computer?
What kind are you going to get?
4 What's Sarah going to do after university?
How long is she going to be away?
5 Are Chris and Kate going to get married?
Where are they going to live?

65
Example answers:
I'm going to listen to some rock music.
I'm not going to spend a lot of money.
My brother is going to play on the computer.
My mother is not going to eat some chocolate.
My friend, Colin, is going to do some work.
I'm going to email some friends.

66
2 's going to have
3 She's going to be
4 He's going to
5 They're going to
6 I'm going to

67
3 No, he won't. He'll probably be in the city centre.
4 *True.*
5 No, he won't. He'll be with his friends.
6 *True.*
7 No, he won't. He'll be 40.
8 No, they won't. They'll probably be at school.
9 He doesn't know where he'll be in 2050.

Example answers:
This evening I'll probably be at home.
Tomorrow morning I'll probably be at school.
Next month I'll be on holiday.
A few years from now I'll probably have a good job.
In 2030 I don't know where I'll be.

68
Example answers:
2 I don't think I'll walk.
I think I'll go by car.
3 I don't think he'll fail (his history exam).
I think he'll pass.
4 I think they'll go to Australia.
I don't think they'll stay in Scotland.
5 I think she'll stay at the garage.
I don't think she'll change jobs.
6 I don't think she'll buy a new computer.
I think she'll keep her old computer.

69
2 Shall I make
3 Shall I close
4 Shall I open/do
5 Shall I turn
6 Shall I take
7 Shall I clean/wash

70
2 Shall we stay
3 Shall we use/take

4 Shall we drive *or* Shall we
go by car
5 shall we go
6 Shall I ask/invite

71

2 are you doing
3 are going
4 will fly
5 shall we go
6 We're not going to camp
7 we'll probably stay
8 We're going to have
9 I'll phone

72

1 It'll probably be about
three hours.
I'm going to the dentist at
5.30.
2 When does the next term
begin?
What are you going to do
during the holidays?
My school doesn't finish
until next week.
Then I'm going to look for
a job for the summer.
3 I'm going to visit my
grandmother.
I'm going to take it to the
garage tomorrow.
I'll lend you mine.
I'll pay for the petrol.

73

3 'm seeing
4 'll make
5 does (the sun) rise
6 are (you) going
7 *OK*
8 'll snow
9 *OK*
10 'll call
11 *OK*

74

2 I'll buy/get you another one.
3 I'm going shopping with
my sister.
4 I'll ring/(tele)phone/call you
this evening.
5 Tony and Rachel are
coming to dinner tonight
6 you'll like it
7 What are you doing
8 I'm going to the seaside

75

2 might take/get a taxi ...
they might not come
3 I might invite/ask Sarah ...
I might not invite/ask Tony
4 She might buy/get some
jeans ... she might not
buy/get anything

76

3 He's going to walk along
the Great Wall.
4 He might go on a boat trip
down the Yangtse River.
5 He's not going to eat
western food.
6 He might try green tea.
7 He's going to learn a little
Chinese.
8 He might not come home.

77

2 can
3 can't
4 can't
5 can't
6 can

8 could see
9 couldn't get
10 couldn't climb
11 couldn't phone
12 could see

78

3 can't cook
4 couldn't sleep
5 couldn't understand
6 can't come
7 couldn't catch
8 couldn't play
9 can't see

79

2 He could play the guitar ...
he couldn't sing.
3 He could swim really well
... he couldn't ride a bike.
4 he can't play the guitar.
5 He can play the piano ... he
can't drive a car.

Example answers:
When I was younger, I could
sleep for a long time. I
couldn't speak English.
Now, I can drive a car. I can't
cook very well.

80

3 Could I borrow a hair
dryer, please?
4 Could you give me a wake-
up call at 6.30 in the
morning, please?
5 Could I have breakfast in
my room tomorrow
morning, please?
6 Could I leave my passport
and traveller's cheques in
the hotel safe, please?
7 Could you get a taxi for
me, please?
(You can also use can *in these
situations.)*

81

2 must study ... mustn't
watch ... don't need to buy
any food / go shopping
3 must take your medicine ...
mustn't get up ... don't
need to eat anything

Example answers:
I must email my friend
because I want to ask him
something.
I mustn't shout at my brother
because he cries when I do.
I don't need to take the dog
for a walk tonight because I
took him this morning.
I don't need to go to the gym
today because I went
yesterday for 2 hours.

82

Example answers:
3 had to work late
4 must go to bed
5 had to stay with a friend
6 had to go to the dentist
7 must hurry

83

2 You should go
You shouldn't eat/have
3 You should take/have
You shouldn't work/read/
use the computer
4 You should tell
You shouldn't lend/give

84

2 Do you think I should ask
3 Do you think I/we should go
4 Do you think I/we should get/buy/have

85

Example answers:
2 I think / I don't think she should go to the party.
  I think / I don't think she should (stay at home and) study.
3 I think / I don't think he should stay at school.
  I think / I don't think he should listen to his parents.
4 I think / I don't think they should be careful with their money.
  I think / I don't think they should go out every night.

86

2 Do I have to write
3 don't have to shout
4 didn't have to choose
5 has to stay
6 didn't have to tell

87

2 Did you have to do
3 did you have to travel
4 don't have to wear
5 had to wear
6 has to work
7 does he have to take
8 has to get
9 didn't have to do
10 had to take

88

2 Don't eat
3 Don't use
4 Wash up
5 Throw the rubbish away
6 Don't play music
7 Lock the door carefully
Example answers:
Clean the shower when you've used it.
Make a cup of coffee for me every evening.
Don't borrow my clothes.
Don't make a noise when you come in.

89

2 Turn
3 Walk
4 Cross
5 Take
6 Ask

Example answer:
Go straight up Banbury Road. Turn left at the cinema. Walk along Stone Avenue and then take the first road on the right. It's called Wessex Street. Cross the road and you'll see the supermarket.

90

Example answers:
2 Don't open
3 Have a piece of *or* Have some
4 Let's not have *or* Don't let's have … Let's go to the new
5 Turn the music down
6 Don't ask me questions

91

2 used to be
3 used to play
4 used to swim/fish
5 used to live
6 used to walk
7 used to eat/cook
8 used to work
9 used to be

Example answers:
I used to go to the park every day.
I used to like drawing.
I used to listen to cassettes.
I used to live in a small village.

92

2 used to live
3 used to hunt
4 wear
5 used to cook
6 used to take off
7 used to spend
8 used to wear
9 ride
10 used to take
11 go
12 used to be
13 hate

93

2 there's
3 it's
4 there's
5 there are
6 Is there
7 there are
8 Are there
9 there aren't
10 Is it
11 There isn't
12 It's

94

2 It's
3 there wasn't
4 it was
5 There's
6 it was
7 it was
8 there was
9 It's
10 There's / There has been
11 it's

95

2 Don't you?
3 Can't he?
4 Did I?
5 Doesn't she?
6 Haven't you?
7 Aren't you?
8 Was he?
9 Were you?
10 Has she?

96

2 didn't you
3 do you
4 haven't you
5 isn't it
6 were they
7 have you

97

2 Tim doesn't have a girlfriend at the moment, but Damian does.
3 Tim was good at school, but Damian wasn't.
4 Tim went to university, but Damian didn't.
5 Tim enjoys listening to other bands, but Damian doesn't.
6 Tim hasn't been to many countries, but Damian has.

98

2 wasn't born
3 didn't live
4 can't speak
5 haven't got
6 isn't
7 don't live
8 won't be

99

4 I do.
5 Neither have I.
6 I'm not.
7 So did I.
8 Neither do I.
9 So will I.

11 neither can Meg
12 neither has Meg
13 so did Meg
14 neither does Meg
15 so will Meg

Example answers:
Julia and Meg can't play
  volleyball and neither can I.
Meg likes jazz and so do I.
Julia and Meg haven't got any
  brothers and neither have I.
Meg isn't looking for a new
  job and neither am I.

100

2 What do you do?
3 Did you go to university?
  or … study at university?
4 Are you married?
5 Where/How did you meet
  your wife?
6 Have you got any
  children? *or* Do you have
  …
7 Does Emily go to school?
8 Does your wife work?
9 Do you enjoy your job?
10 How much holiday do
  you have/get?

101

3 are you going to say
4 happened
5 likes
6 told
7 's playing

102

2 does she come from? *or* is
  she from?
3 's she waiting for?
4 's she talking to?
5 did it belong to?
6 's he looking at?
7 are they talking about?

103

1 Where did you … Who did
  you … What was
2 What have you … How did
  you … Does it
3 What time does it … How
  long does it … Which
  jacket shall I

104

2 Why didn't you ring me last
  night?
3 Who are you giving that
  present to?
4 How much has Mary
  spent?
5 Where did Jo go for her
  holidays last year?
6 How long does it take to
  get to your school?
7 What do you usually do in
  the evenings?
8 What happened yesterday
  evening?
9 When was the Taj Mahal
  built?

105

2 What do you want to see?
3 Have you seen it?
4 Who did you go with?
5 What was it like?
6 would you like to do
  something else?
7 Why don't you come to
  my house?
8 How long are they going
  to be away?
9 Can I bring anything for
  dinner?
10 What do you want to talk
  to me about?
11 how long does it take to
  walk to your house from
  the station? *or* … from
  the station to your house?

106

2 I don't know if he'll go and
  work abroad.
3 I don't know if his fiancée
  is Spanish.
4 I don't know where he met
  this wonderful woman.
5 I don't know how long
  they've known each other.
6 I don't know when the
  wedding is.
7 I don't know if we're
  invited.

107

2 Do you know what he was
  wearing?
3 Do you know who was
  with him? *or* … who he
  was with?
4 Do you know how much
  it / the camera cost?
5 Do you know what kind of
  shop he went into? *or* Do
  you know which shop …
6 Do you know why the
  person (with him) was
  laughing?
7 Do you know where the
  train was going to?

108

2 Do you know why all the
  shops are closed today?
3 Do you know where the
  Regent Hotel is?
4 Do you know how much
  the tickets cost/are?
5 Do you know when Mr
  Collins died?
6 Do you know if there's a
  Chinese restaurant nearby /
  near here?

109

Example answers:
Do you know if the subway
  closes at night?
Do you know if you can go
  up the Statue of Liberty?
Do you know what's on at the
  theatre?
Do you know where I can buy
  some stamps?

110

3 he had (got) a few days' holiday
4 (he) was going to Italy
5 he was ill
6 (he) had been in bed for two days
7 she didn't like parties
8 (she) couldn't dance
9 his sister was arriving from Australia on Saturday
10 he was going to meet her at the airport
11 she loved parties
12 (she) would be free on Saturday

111

2 Paul said you didn't work here on Mondays.
3 Stuart said you'd gone out.
4 Simon said you were at lunch and (you) would be back soon.
5 Mike said you left early on Mondays.
6 Diana said you were making a cup of tea.
7 Mary said she didn't know (where you were).

Example answer:
8 I was in the chairman's office.

112

2 A
3 B
4 C
5 B
6 B
7 C
8 C
9 C
10 C

113

3 to go
4 to be
5 to tell
6 to drive
7 to let
8 to do
9 slowing
10 to see
11 to come
12 talking

13 to go
14 writing

114

2 told David not to play with that knife
3 didn't let his young sons play with toy guns
4 persuaded Jane to come swimming with us
5 didn't expect you to fail the exam *or* expected you to pass
6 made me pay back all the money I (had) borrowed

115

2 do
3 do
4 doing
5 to do
6 doing
7 to do

Example answers:
2 They made me go to bed early.
3 They never let me go to other children's houses.
4 I don't mind washing the dishes.
5 I've always wanted to learn to dive.
6 I most enjoy watching a video or DVD.
7 I'd like to be a doctor.

116

Example answers:
3 invite her to my party.
4 some information.
5 to pay the bills / for my holiday.
6 to make a cup of coffee / for a knife.
7 to finish her work / for sport.
8 to see the new Disney film / for a letter.

117

The correct answers are:
2 doesn't mind / likes
3 made / let
4 use / learn
5 started / suggested
6 forgot / don't need
7 told / advised

118

3 holding
4 having
5 to swim
6 to bring
7 leaving
8 to go
9 do
10 to go
11 to study
12 telling

119

3 do
4 made
5 made
6 make
7 makes
8 made
9 do
10 doing
11 do
12 to do
13 made
14 do
15 making
16 do *or* to do
17 did
18 did
19 to do

120

2 Do you have a temperature? *or* Have you got …
3 What are we going to have for lunch today? *or* What are we having …
4 Can you have a look at my computer? *or* Could you …
5 How many jobs have you had?
6 Shall we have a walk later?

121

2 him
3 I
4 We
5 It
6 me
7 he
8 them
9 they
10 its
11 my
12 our

122

13 My
14 his
15 their
16 her

122

2 you
3 your
4 me
5 my
6 mine
7 They
8 them
9 I
10 her
11 us
12 his
13 he
14 him
15 him
16 them
17 Their
18 hers
19 mine
20 yours
21 their
22 your

123

4 by herself
5 each other
6 myself
7 each other

124

2 cut themselves
3 understand each other
4 went by herself
5 enjoyed ourselves
6 wrote ... each other

125

3 James gave me those books. I really like them.
4 Some friends of theirs told them the news.
5 Pat gave her brother a DVD and he gave her a book.
6 My sister and her husband don't love each other any more. They aren't happy together.
7 John is a good friend of mine.
8 OK

9 I like this house but its windows are broken.
10 I know Mary, but I don't know her brother.
11 I sometimes ask myself why I work in a noisy city.

126

2 Anne's car
3 Elena's house
4 the students' books
5 my sister's birthday
6 Mrs Penn's cakes
7 grandparents' house
8 Chris's parents

127

2 The computer games are Alan's
3 The books are Alan's.
4 The football is Mike's.
5 The chocolates are Mike's. *or* The box of chocolates is Mike's.
6 The (running) shoes are Alan's.
7 The guitar is Alan's.
8 The magazine is Mike's.

128

3 John's favourite team
4 the result of the match
5 your parents' anniversary party
6 the windows of the house
7 the telephone number of the station
8 Mark Turner's daughter

129

2 an empty glass
3 a difficult question
4 an old book
5 a hot day
6 a cheap hotel
7 a young man
8 a heavy bag
9 an interesting film

130

2 watches
3 tomatoes
4 feet
5 teeth
6 women
7 children

8 babies
9 sheep
10 days

131

The correct answers are:
2 A
3 A / C
4 B / C
5 A
6 A
7 C
8 A / B

132

1 some suntan oil
2 some CDs
  a CD player
  some perfume / a bottle of perfume
  a pair of sunglasses
3 some books
  a pair of jeans
  some face cream
  a map
4 two pairs of trousers
  some/three T-shirts
  some money
  a (rain)coat/jacket

Example answers:
a camera, a guidebook, a sunhat, a dictionary, a pair of walking boots, some books

133

2 a (musician) ... the (best)
3 an (idea) ... the (new)
4 the (station) ... a (taxi) ... the (city centre)
5 the (kitchen) ... a (guest) ... the (dining room)
6 the (capital) ... a (large)
7 the (third) ... an (old)
8 a (large) ... the (middle) ... the (country) ... a (dog) ... the (dog)
9 the (same) ... an (older) ... the (most)
10 the (nearest) ... the (end) ... the (left) ... a (bus stop)

134

3 the station manager
4 an Italian restaurant
5 the left

6 the Information Centre
7 the restaurant
8 a woman
9 the kitchen
10 the man
11 *OK*
12 the same
13 the papers
14 the police
15 *OK*
16 the table

135
3 –
4 the
5 –
6 the
7 –
8 the
9 –
10 –
11 the
12 –
13 –
14 –
15 –

136
2 –
3 the
4 –
5 the
6 the
7 –
8 –
9 –

137
2 any
3 some
4 some
5 some
6 any
7 some
8 any
9 some
10 any

138
2 something
3 someone/somebody
4 something
5 anyone/anybody
6 something
7 anything
8 Someone/Somebody
9 anything

139
2 haven't got any money / don't have any money *or* have (got) no money
3 haven't got any chocolates / don't have any chocolates *or* have (got) no chocolates
4 aren't any (biscuits) *or* are no biscuits
5 isn't any milk *or* 's no milk
6 haven't got any food / don't have any food *or* have (got) no food
7 isn't any time *or* 's no time

140
2 any
3 None
4 *OK*
5 any
6 any
7 *OK*
8 no
9 some

141
2 None
3 no
4 any
5 Some
6 no
7 some
8 any
9 any
10 some

142
2 nowhere
3 nothing
4 someone/somebody
5 somewhere
6 No-one/Nobody
7 someone/somebody
8 anything
9 something
10 anywhere

143
2 something to eat
3 nothing to do
4 anyone/anybody to play
5 anywhere to stay
6 something to wear
7 anything to say / to talk about

144
2 all
3 all
4 Every
5 all
6 every
7 all

145
2 Everyone/Everybody
3 everything
4 everywhere
5 everywhere
6 everyone/everybody

146
2 –
3 of
4 of
5 –
6 –
7 –
8 of
9 of
10 –
11 of

147
2 Some of Richard's colleagues walk to work. *or* Some of them walk …
3 All (of) Richard's colleagues have (got) a car. *or* All of them have …
4 Most of Richard's colleagues use their car every day. *or* Most of them use …
5 Some of Lisa's friends go to the cinema every month.
6 All (of) Lisa's friends play some kind of sport. *or* All of them play …
7 None of Lisa's friends study every night. *or* None of them study …
8 Most of Lisa's friends enjoy dancing. *or* Most of them enjoy …

Example answers
All of us take regular exercise.
Most of us play some kind of sport.
Some of us enjoy dancing.
None of us study every night.

148
2 Neither
3 either
4 Both
5 Both of
6 either of
7 Neither

149

Example answers:
Both of us like dancing.
Neither of us has got a brother.
Both of us go to the gym every day.
Neither of us is married.
Both of us have to learn English.
Neither of us drives a car.

150

2 There isn't much champagne.
3 There isn't any orange juice.
4 There isn't much cake.
5 There aren't any sandwiches.
6 There isn't much fish.
7 There aren't many cherries.

151

2 How much milk do you like in your coffee? (A lot. / Not (very) much. / A little. / None.)
3 How many cars can you see out of the window? (A lot. / Not (very) many. / A few / None.)
4 How much money do you spend in one month? (A lot. / Not (very) much. / A little. / None.)
5 How many good friends do you have? (A lot. / Not (very) many. / A few. / None.)
6 How much water do you drink every day? (A lot. / Not (very) much. / A little. / None.)
7 How many pairs of socks do you have? (A lot. / Not (very) many. / A few. / None.)

152

2 a few   5 little
3 a few   6 a little
4 little

153

2 old hotel
3 hot water

4 famous places/sights
5 delicious food/meals
6 friendly people
7 difficult language
8 busy roads/streets/towns
9 big country/place

154

2 happy   8 carefully
3 good   9 well
4 well   10 delicious
5 good   11 badly
6 brilliantly   12 hard
7 fantastic   13 quickly

155

2 than   8 colder/worse
3 more   9 as
4 as   10 as
5 as   11 more
6 more   12 than
7 more

(Use the paragraphs about the USA and Australia to help you with your answer.)

156

4 Life is more expensive than it was.
5 People are not as friendly as they were.
6 Films are more violent than they were.
7 People live longer than they did.
8 Houses are better than they were.
9 Families are not as big as they were.
10 Children have (got) more freedom than they had.
11 People eat better food than they did.

157

2 B, C, A: The python is the longest snake and the rattlesnake is longer than the cobra.
3 B, A, C: Antarctica is the coldest place and Scotland is colder than France.
4 A, C, B: The cheetah is the fastest animal and the lion is faster than the mouse.

5 C, B, A: 'Of' is the most common preposition in English and 'at' is more common than 'into'.
6 A, C, B: The Great White Shark is the most dangerous creature and the scorpion is more dangerous than the cockroach.

158

2 Who's the most interesting person you've ever met?
3 What's the most frightening experience you've ever had?
4 What's the worst film you've ever seen?
5 What's the most expensive thing you've ever bought?
6 What's the most unusual food you've ever eaten?
7 Which is the largest city you've ever visited?

159

2 Jo lives much <u>further</u> away now.
3 My mum is the same age <u>as</u> my dad.
4 *OK*
5 This is the <u>oldest</u> house in the city.
6 Traffic in the city is <u>worse</u> in the evenings.
7 This dictionary is <u>the</u> best I've ever had.
8 Paul isn't as lazy <u>as</u> he seems.
9 *OK*
10 Meg is the <u>most</u> intelligent person in her family.
11 It's not as <u>warm</u> as it was yesterday.
12 This is the <u>most comfortable</u> chair in the room.

160

2 Have you got <u>enough money</u> to pay for the tickets?
3 Have you got <u>enough information</u> to answer the question?

4 Has he worked <u>hard enough</u> to pass his exams?

5 Are there <u>enough plates</u> for everyone?

6 Is your tea <u>sweet enough</u> or would you <u>like</u> some more sugar?

161

2 sharp enough to cut
3 enough money to buy
4 well enough to go
5 enough time to answer/do
6 warm enough to play

162

2 ate/had too many chocolates
3 is too much traffic *or* are too many cars
4 are too many people
5 is too hot
6 drank/had too much coffee

163

3 There aren't enough cinemas.
4 There's too much noise and dirt.
5 The parks are too small. *or* The parks aren't big enough.
6 There aren't enough things to do in the evenings.
7 There are too many tourists.

Example answers:
There are too many cars and not enough parking spaces.
There aren't enough tennis courts.
The shops aren't open long enough.
There's too much noise in the city centre.

164

3 No, they're not old enough to get married. *or* they're too young to …
4 Yes, he's old enough to drive a car.
5 No, she's not old enough to buy a dog. *or* she's too young to …

6 Yes, he's old enough to leave school.
7 No, she's too young to vote. *or* she's not old enough to …

165

2 Maria rarely goes to bed before midnight.
3 I've got lots of friends, but they are all on holiday at the moment.
4 I like chocolate very much.
5 When do you usually do your homework?
6 I can never remember my car registration number.
7 Carmen always arrives home late from work.
8 Clare is a good piano player. She's also learning to play the guitar.
9 John and Steve? They are both living in Brazil now.
10 José finished his exams yesterday.

166

2 'm still looking for … haven't found them yet
3 's still raining … haven't seen the sun yet
4 haven't got up yet … 'm still in bed
5 hasn't apologised yet … 'm still angry
6 'm still driving … haven't bought a new car yet

167

3 but
4 and
5 or
6 but
7 so
8 and (*but* is also possible)
9 so
10 because (but *is also possible*)
11 so
12 or
13 and
14 because

168

3 while you were at work
4 until you're better
5 when I'm speaking on the phone
6 When I finish college
7 While I was walking home
8 before we leave the house
9 When I heard the news
10 when I'm in town

169

2 we're
3 we miss the beginning of
4 we don't understand
5 we're bored
6 we fall asleep

170

2 if I <u>had</u> one
3 if she <u>weren't/wasn't</u> ill
4 it <u>doesn't</u> rain
5 you <u>found</u>
6 he <u>got up</u>
7 he <u>won't</u> tell

171

3 If I weren't/wasn't (so) busy at college, I'd go on holiday.
4 If it had a bigger memory, I'd buy it.
5 I wouldn't buy it if I were/was you.
6 We'll miss the train if he doesn't arrive soon.

172

3 which crashed into mine was green
4 's the newspaper which was on the table
5 which was left on the bus yesterday belongs to
6 spoke to an assistant who had long, dark hair
7 writes books which are translated into many languages
8 who went to last night's concert enjoyed it

173

2 worked in was called 'Bangles'
3 was watching on TV were playing in a river
4 of the friends Sally stayed with
5 Kate went on holiday with live in the same street
6 I'm reading was written over 300 years ago
7 you were waiting for arrive
8 man Fiona's playing tennis with

174

2 who/that wrote over 100 books
3 (which/that) we went to see last week
4 (who/that) I told you about
5 (which/that) she started
6 which/that gave me the money to study in America
7 who/that made tennis popular
8 who/that had six wives

175

2 at midnight
3 on 22 November 1963
4 at night
5 in winter
6 at 6.30 am
7 in 1920
8 at the weekend
9 on Thursday morning

176

2	before	10	after
3	In	11	in
4	at	12	on
5	in	13	in
6	After/In	14	in
7	From	15	Since
8	to/until	16	for
9	In		

177

2	to/until	7	before
3	During	8	since
4	After	9	until
5	while		
6	for		

12 on
13 After
14 in
15 from
16 to/until
17 until
18 at
19 for
20 At
21 while
22 Before
23 until
24 since
25 In
26 At

(Use the paragraphs about Jess Brewer to help you with your answer)

178

2 It's on the left, on the top shelf, between the pasta and the bread.
3 They're on the right, on the bottom shelf, opposite the nuts.
4 It's on the right, on the middle shelf, next to the cola.
5 It's on the right, on the top shelf, above the cola.
6 They're below the cola, on the bottom shelf, in the middle, between the biscuits and the chocolate.

Example answers:

7 It's on the right, on the top shelf, opposite the bread.
8 It's on the left, on the middle shelf, in the middle, between the sugar and the eggs.

179

2	at	9	in
3	in	10	to
4	at	11	to
5	to	12	to
6	at	13	to
7	in	14	–
8	at		

180

3 past/(a)round
4 along/down
5 (a)round
6 under
7 on/onto
8 on
9 off
10 out of
11 through
12 across
13 into
14 over

181

2 are different from the ones/apples you bought yesterday
3 'm not interested in rugby
4 'm fed up with (the) rain
5 is afraid of storms
6 isn't very good at cooking
7 is nice to her elderly neighbours
8 is full of furniture
9 are you angry with Liz?

182

2 about/for not writing
3 of/about leaving
4 in selling
5 with saying
6 of being
7 at selling

183

2	to	8	for
3	about	9	to
4	to	10	with
5	at	11	at
6	–	12	for
7	for	13	to

184

2 up … off … away/off
3 off/away … back
4 down
5 over … on
6 up … on … up
7 down … in

185

2 switch / turn the light on *or* switch / turn on the light
3 Put your glasses on
4 give it / the money back (to you) *or* give (you) back the money
5 pick it / the magazine up *or* pick up the magazine
6 turn it / your music / the music / down *or* turn down your/the music
7 turn it off
8 throw them away/out

Thanks

The authors would like to thank Alison Sharpe and Jessica Roberts of Cambridge University Press for advice and support, and Liz Driscoll for her helpful suggestions and great editing. Also, everyone at Kamae for their creative design work.

Photo Acknowledgements
The publishers are grateful to the following for permission to reproduce copyright photographs and material:

Key: l = left, c = centre, r = right, t = top, b = bottom

Alamy Images/©Tibor Bognar for p 11; Art Directors & TRIP for p 108; Corbis/©John Springer Collection for p 20, /©Royalty Free for p 29, /©Bill Varie for p 48, /©Hans Strand for p 85, /©Goegel/Zefa for p 93; Getty Images for pp 7(t), 7(b), 32, 74, 99; Photolibrary/©The Travel Library Ltd for p 9; Punchstock/©PhotoAlto for p 8; Rex Features for pp 35, 43, 49.

Picture Research by Hilary Luckcock.